LIFE BEYOND DEATH

LIFE BEYOND DEATH

A Christian Response to Bereavement

Rosalyn A. Kendrick

The Canterbury Press
Norwich

© Rosalyn A. Kendrick 1995

First published 1995 by The Canterbury Press Norwich
(a publishing imprint of Hymns Ancient & Modern Limited,
a registered charity)
St Mary's Works, St Mary's Plain,
Norwich, Norfolk, NR3 3BH

British Library Cataloguing in Publication Data

A catalogue record for this book is available
from the British Library

ISBN 1-85311-102-3

*Typeset by Datix International Limited
Bungay, Suffolk and
Printed and bound in Great Britain by
Bell and Bain Ltd. Glasgow*

'For God so loved the world that He gave
His only Son, that whoever believes in him
should not perish but have
eternal life.'   (John 3.16)

FOREWORD

by Michael Perry

Sub-Dean of Durham Cathedral and
consulting editor of the *Journal of Near-Death Studies*

Why is death still – so often, to so many people, even to Christians – the great unmentionable? Why, when the only certain thing about anyone's life is that it is bound to end?

Perhaps, as T. S. Eliot wistfully remarked, it is because 'humankind cannot bear too much reality'.

I am glad that Rosalyn Kendrick has written this book. Too many unthinking Christians believe that grief is a sign of unbelief; it is much more a sign of the deepest ties of love in a situation of anguish. Too many unthinking Christians have got pat answers to the problems of miscarriage, or abortion, or stillbirth. Reality, as Rosalyn Kendrick knows, is never as tidy as all that.

This book is well-grounded both in a deep knowledge of the teachings of all three of the great monotheistic world faiths, and is fully aware of recent studies of near-death experiences; but, more importantly, it is not a theoretical account. It springs from its author's life-experiences. Therefore, without sentimentality but with gentle persistence, it sets out what believers in God can say, and think, and do – about their own certain deaths, and about the deaths of loved ones, and about their own and others' bereavements.

I welcome this book and commend it to all who are bereaved, to all who wish to comfort the bereaved, and to all who have the courage to contemplate their own mortality.

MICHAEL PERRY
Durham, September 1994

CONTENTS

Acknowledgements

The author and publisher are grateful to the following for granting permission to quote extracts from copyright material: Lion Publishing plc, *Face to Face with Cancer* by Marion Stroud, *The Long Road Ahead* by W. Green, and *What Happens After Death?* by David Winter; S.C.M. Press Ltd, *The Many Faces of Grief* by Edgar N. Jackson, 1977; Fontana, an imprint of HarperCollins Publishers Limited, *Men and Divorce* by J. Abulafia, 1990; Edward Robinson, *Angels in Dark Places* by B. Statham (and included in *The Original Vision* by Alister Hardy Research Unit); MBB Inc, *Life After Life* by Raymond A. Moody.

The author has endeavoured to obtain permission for the use of copyright material but in cases of oversight or error, offers sincere apologies and undertakes to acknowledge in a future edition.

Awareness of Mortality

There comes a day in the life of all people when they are obliged to live with the knowledge that they are going to die.

Death, and bereavement through death, has to be faced as a fact of life. We cannot prevent it. It makes no difference if we have avoided the thought before; we always hope that death will not happen to us, will not disrupt our family, our marriage – but of course we know in our hearts that there is no avoiding it. We know that from the moment we are conceived our life is a journey, one that will come to an end. In fact, we could say that from the moment of our conception, we are dying. The fact that we will die is the ONLY fact we can know for sure about our own futures. It is a sobering thought.

As young people we all spend time wondering what we will do when we 'grow up', what we will achieve, what successes we will have. We all have a tendency to assume that we WILL grow up. We forget that no one has the right to assume that they will live three-score years and ten, and die in the fullness of old age. Indeed, we have not the slightest idea of what it is that will kill us – whether we will succumb to some unpleasant disease, or die in perfect health – catching a bullet in war, perishing in fire or flood, being caught out by some accident.

The notion that any human being can *know* what lies ahead of them is completely false, an illusion. I often used to ask my young students how many of them knew what they were going to have for their evening meal, or how they were going to get home after the class. Most of them would put up their hands with a confident answer. Only a few would hesitate, knowing that I have a fondness for 'trick questions'. The next question, of course, was how many of them actually knew they *would* be having their evening meal, or would be arriving at their homes for sure? This time, the raised hands were quavering a little – they were not so confident.

For the truth, as opposed to the illusion, is that *no person knows their future*, what will happen in the next minute, never mind the next evening or the next day.

This, actually, is God's will for us. We are not *meant* to know. Some people claim that they can find out what future events are going to come to pass by psychic means. Perhaps some crystal-gazer has told them that they will die on a particular date. It is important to realise that such future–predictors have omitted to recognise a big catch in their arguments. In fact, their confidence can make them highly dangerously negative practitioners, for the ability to make accurate future predictions carries with it the serious flaw of esoteric fatalism, which has quite justifiably caused thousands of people to fear astrologers and numerologists.

Any clairvoyant predicting a future disastrous or fatal event plants a negative seed in the mind of the individual, a subtle form of hypnosis that may sometimes have the power to cause things to happen which would never have happened without the prediction. It is quite possible for future-predictors to be the direct cause of unnecessary deaths, simply by programming them into the trusting minds of those they advise.

For example, the astrologer Cheiro claimed great skill in predicting future events, and had several sessions with King Edward VII of England. He predicted his death for May 6th in his 69th year. He *repeatedly* made this fatal prediction, backing it up with examples of his other 'successes'; the King even jokingly referred to him as 'the man who won't let me live past 69!' However, on the due date, the King suddenly became ill, and died. Cheiro claimed it as a 'success', but the fact is that the King had been powerfully hypnotised, his subconscious deeply programmed with the negative seed – and so, he obliged. (For this case, refer to Linda Goodman's *Star Signs*, Pan, 1987, pp215–217).

A basic concept

One of the basic concepts of religion is that only God, the Almighty Creator, has the full knowledge of our futures and our fates. He alone knows the answer to every single thing; and our share of that knowledge is no more nor less than He chooses to reveal to us.

'Then the Lord answered Job out of the whirlwind: "Who is this that darkens counsel by words without knowledge? ... Where were you when I laid the foundations of the Earth?"' (Job 38. 1–4)

The biblical saga of the Book of Job is a full outline of the philosophy that humans are tested by God in all sorts of ways, including sickness, loss of fortune, disease and death. All humans come under this test, no matter how saintly they happen to be. Job was a very saintly man yet he suffered terribly in his lifetime, even though he could think of no sin for which to repent. Because of his saintliness, he refused to curse God, but 'patiently' accepted his sufferings as part of God's will, and did his best not to feel resentful. At the end of the book he was granted an 'interview' with God, who pointed out to him that patience and acceptance were the correct attitude when confronted with inexplicable shifts of fortune, since no human being could possibly know the Truth about God, or His motivation. The 'full story' lies entirely beyond human experience. Job accepted this, and in his acceptance of God's will for him, God changed his circumstances and his fortunes were unexpectedly restored anew.

Unfortunately, thanks to the ceaseless bombardment of the western mind with media material that suggests happy endings for all dramas, eleventh-hour reprieves, miraculous interventions and so forth, many Christians have lost sight of this important and basic attitude of faith.

No human person has the right to assume that God will intervene and take away miraculously the suffering and the test and the mortality of an individual – no matter how noble that soul. One has only to think of the desperate prayer of Jesus in the Garden of Gethsemane, when he prayed so earnestly that he might have 'this cup (i.e. his terrible approaching death) removed from him' that his sweat broke out of him like drops of blood (Luke 22. 44). Even in his case, the experience of death was not to be avoided, and he concluded his prayer in acceptance – 'Not my will but Thine be done'.

Many people watched him die, laughing at his fate, tormenting him by challenging him to come down off the cross. They tried to make the point that if he really was the Son of God,

Life Beyond Death

then God would save him. The Christian faith is built up on the belief that God *did not save him*; and he died. There was no miracle of intervention, even for him. However, there was the greater miracle – the demonstration that even though we have to pass through death, DEATH IS NOT THE END.

The fact of the human lack of knowledge, and the importance of faith and acceptance of God's will, are very important points to take into account when we are confronted with the trauma of what seems to be a 'medical death-sentence'. Only a person who has actually gone through the horror of discovering they have an incurable disease can fully understand the dreadful terror of that moment; the cold claws grasping the pit of the stomach, the nausea and shock. Those who have not had this experience can murmur their sympathy, but they cannot really *feel* it.

Once the 'bombshell' has been dropped, it has a devastating effect on the person involved. The automatic tendency, of course, is to react violently and passionately, out of shock – how can this be true? How can this happen to me? Oh my God, I'm going to die! Panic sets in, and fear. Inevitably, this panic leads to depression and despair, and the future outlook for someone in this state is very bleak indeed. Whatever time they have left, they are now obliged to spend it with the clock ticking loudly in the background. Suddenly, the rest of one's life is not just that – an unknown future still full of possibilities and ambitions to be realised, but 'the amount of time I have left'.

This is where the faith of the believer is so important, and can make such a vital difference. The believer knows that the knowledge of the human is limited. Imagine two people, two women, sitting together in a hospital canteen – one has just been told that she has an incurable cancer, and the other that her pregnancy test has proved positive and she will bear a longed-for child. The face of the one is grey and drawn, the soul heavy and the expression bleak; the more fortunate woman is radiant and glowing, full of excitement and high hopes. They finish their tea, and step out together into the bright sunlight of the street outside. Life seems to be holding out to them such different fortunes, and we rejoice with the bearer of new life and shrink sadly away from the woman smitten with disease, not knowing how to console her.

In fact, our pity and our envy are quite misplaced, and based on our human ignorance. Things do not turn out as imagined. The woman with cancer responds well to treatment and lives another twenty years, whereas the healthy, pregnant young woman dies in a road-accident within the week.

Let me give a personal example. Rather late in life I made a second marriage to a man considerably younger than myself. I used to be tormented by worries as to what would happen to him when I died, always assuming that because of our age difference I would leave this earth long before him. My husband used to get quite angry with me, and point out that since he was the driver of our car and frequently went on long journeys when he was tired he was far more likely to die before me. Neither of us can possibly know who will go first. We have an equal chance.

Seems strange, doesn't it? But life's like that!

Learn to recognise shock

We have to learn to recognise shock, and then to tackle it in faith, if possible. Here's a little more of a personal nature from my own experiences. I hope that it is obvious from what I have written above that I have some faith in God and His overlooking of our situation. Even so, I have had the experience of being confronted by death from cancer several times. Each time I went through the most horrible and appalling shock and fear symptoms.

Each experience was different, and involved people with whom I had differing relationships. My first case was my grandfather, whom I can barely remember now. I know he retired from the Royal Air Force after serving all his life, and almost immediately went down with cancer. I remember how no one ever spoke depressingly to him, but talked of what they would do when he was better. I, a small child, thought the grown-ups must really be daft if they really thought he was going to get better – it seemed so obvious to me that he was getting weaker and worse. I was rarely on my own with Grandad, but when I was, I suffered awful embarrassment and dismay, because I did not know what to say to him, or how to talk to him. I suppose I realised that people kept on saying bright things because they didn't know what to say either. He faced his increasing illness and approaching death as bravely and stoically as he faced everything else in life, and as far as I know, he never admitted the truth that he was going to die to anyone either. Everyone kept up the bluff. In the end, he died in his sleep, from what we all believed was a massive overdose of morphine administered in order to have that effect and release him from his suffering.

My second case was that of a dearly-loved aunt, the person to whom I felt closest in all the world. She had been a soldier in the First World War and was a 'tough-guy', smoking a large number of cigarettes per day (although she claimed that she never inhaled them! I didn't believe her, she always seemed to have a 'fag' dangling). While I was away at university she went down with lung cancer, and died after quite a long battle. I think we almost accepted this as inevitable, after all her smoking, but we felt very helpless and sad, for she had never been an invalid all her life. My mother did the bulk of the nursing, and it was particularly sad to see a grand old lady who I had always thought of as an exceptionally kind and saintly person who had never complained or been a nuisance all her life, go rapidly downhill and become bedbound and occasionally awkward. As I was away, I was spared the stresses of watching her deterioration, but I grieved for her most bitterly, and still do. I was not there when she died, and I never forgave myself for that. I was also not able to go to her funeral, and that was hard to forgive myself for too. My biggest consolation is that she was a lady of enormous faith in God, and did not fear death. I never think of her as being dead; if I have a departed loved-one's soul taking the role of my guardian angel, I am sure it is her.

My third case was my mother-in-law, an elderly lady, whom I loved in a general sense but with whom I did not have a particularly close relationship. My reaction to her news was one of rather impersonal sympathy, coupled with considerable admiration for the way she 'took it on the chin' and admitted that she thought she had had cancer for some time. She accepted that she had lived a pretty full life, and that she would 'have to go sometime'. She had been a nurse herself and knew what was coming. Even so, she did not seem to be needing any great show of sympathy (just the family's support), and just carried on living calmly, accepting what the medics did to her and appearing to take it all in her stride. If she suffered mental agonies, I did not know. As it happened, in her case the treatment was very successful, and despite losing a breast and having various operations on her face, she went on to live another fifteen years, finally leaving this world in her eighties.

The fourth case was my own. I discovered a lump in my breast and this time had the experience for myself of going to the doctor and being told that it might well be something to worry about. At last, I realised what those other two people had faced. Despite all my boasted faith, I instantly felt very green and sick and had to leave the doctor to rush off to the loo, to throw up, and then to try to pull myself together. My legs went completely to jelly, and I could feel my heart pounding. Doing my best to swallow my fear and behave with dignity, I went back before the doctor, and was told that I could be tested on the National Health but I would not be able to be seen for about two months. If I went privately, things would be dealt with much more quickly. I found the money, and feeling so guilty at my fears and my 'queue-jumping', I hurried to a private consultant. He fixed me up with a quick hospital visit, and a very painful mammogram. Even so, it was over six weeks of nail-biting before I was given the result, which was an all-clear.

My fifth case was my dear sister, whose breast-lump felt quite different from mine – it was hard and pronounced. It proved to be a malignant cancer. This time, I understood exactly the shock and trauma the patient went through, and did my best to be more fully supportive. I certainly understood much better, after my personal shock, the need for contact, telephone calls, consistent support, and not just the one-off pat on the arm and gentle word followed by embarrassed withdrawal. Happily, in her case, after surgery and chemotherapy and homeopathy and diet, the cancer was cured.

My sixth case was that of my little niece, a keen athlete just entering her teenage and already an excellent runner and horse-woman. A suspicious lump on her knee which everyone thought was caused somehow by her riding equipment chafing there, failed to heal. After a long time, the doctor at the surgery decided to open it up and take a look, and to our absolute horror it turned out to be a major cancerous tumor – which was removed without proper anaesthetic in the doctor's surgery. My niece was then rushed off to hospital where she faced further drastic surgery and chemotherapy – but, as with my sister, the cancer has gone and she is once again excelling in her sports. She has also become a very mature, tough and understanding young woman in the process.

My seventh and final case was that of my ex-husband, who had always had a very fair skin (easily affected by sunburn) and many large dark pigment-moles all over his body. He developed melanoma (skin cancer) for which the suggested cause was his time of service in Suez, thirty years previously. He had operations, but he finally succumbed to cancer of the liver. His case was interesting in that he refused nearly all orthodox medical treatment (as he had done all his life, on principle) preferring to treat himself with homeopathy and vitamins. In his case, it did not pay off – and indeed it caused some stress to relatives who had less faith in alternative medicine, who would have preferred him to have accepted more treatment, and who were naturally powerless to intervene or make him change his mind away from what he believed to be the right thing. And who knows, of course?

On this road of human life there are so many fears – fear of losing control, fear of doing the wrong thing and making a fatal error, fear of pain, fear of indignity, and the ultimate terror, fear of giving up the self at the moment of death. We need not torment ourselves with guilt if we react with shock and fear – for this is natural. Even the example of Jesus showed that it was natural. Jesus reacted with horror and dismay just the same as we all do, whether we show it or not – yet God is there.

There are so many questions. Will it be painful? Will we be alone? What will happen after death? Will we find eternal bliss, or be snuffed out? Or perhaps, will we face terrible eternal torments for our sins and weaknesses? Will we find those we have loved who have died before us, waiting for us to welcome us into their celestial company? Or will we change completely, so that we will hardly know ourselves, let alone other people?

Contemplating death is not a pleasant prospect, yet when death has been faced and accepted it has a very dramatic effect upon our outlook to life. A person who has been 'touched' by death can never be the same again. Whether it is facing up to the loss of some dearly-loved relative or friend, or being so ill oneself that one is merging more with the 'afterlife' than the life of this world, once awareness of mortality has entered the human consciousness the human changes, and the attitude to those loved ones also changes. The possibility of losing life makes everything we love and have so much more precious.

We are haunted by the thought that the end of our earthly lives may leave unfinished tasks, incomplete relationships; we are anxious about those we will leave behind who depend upon us. How will they survive without us? What will they do? How will they cope?

A death is a prolonged emotional crisis. At the very least, the circumstances of life of the bereaved change radically. At worst, they feel the meaning of life is lost and its structure shattered.

We know, of course, that we will die, that we will cease to be – but we have one very strong human failing; we like to think we are in control of our own lives and fates. When death strikes, the individual can no longer maintain the illusion of being inviolable, nor believe in the medical experts as omnipotent rescuers who come (like the 'saviour-heros' of films and TV) to put everything right at the last moment and dramatically save us from our fate.

To face this helplessness, and accept it, is very frightening. Many people, on being made to realise that they are soon to die, are quite appalled and indignant. They protest, in agonies of outrage. Why me? Why should this happen to me? In the crisis of facing up to death, people often become understandably selfish and self-centred – as if the possibility of death should happen to everyone else, to other people's loved ones and friends, in other people's villages and streets – but not to THEM!

They have a gut reaction that something very unfair is happening to them – they have done 'nothing wrong', but 'God has picked them out' for punishment. They take the point of view that God has spotted them as individuals and marked them off for death, perhaps because of something they have done . . . it takes time to assimilate the fact that EVERY-BODY has to face death sooner or later, that death is the most natural thing in the world and comes to all.

They have to face their own mortality and make sense of the apparent meaninglessness of life. Without faith, this is doubly difficult, for without an afterlife to make sense of one's earthly life, life IS meaningless. A bereaved person has to make this strongest possible demand on individual adjustment at the very time when he or she feels most exhausted and over-whelmed. Without faith, it is a cruel task indeed.

In fact, there is only one way in which a believer should wish to contemplate death, and that is in the aspect of faith and love. The whole basis for the true life of faith is ACCEPT-ANCE – acceptance of the will of God in every aspect of life; in the home, at work, in the bosom of the family, at war, at business – in everything. When a person is so committed in love to our dear Lord, the various aspects of our mortality are accepted for what they are and not given undue influence over us.

It does not matter if we do not know what our future is going to be – God knows it, and our lives and souls are in His 'hands'. It does not matter if we cannot work out how to appease our ambitions; as long as we do our best, God knows and understands everything. It does not matter if we do not know how long our lives will be – whether we will die old or young; it does not matter what our circumstances are, or in what place or country we are called to live out our spans – God is everywhere and sees everything.

If we have faith, the knowledge of the inevitability of death and bereavement should not be seen as a horrible threat looming over us, but as an important part of our lives, for which we can prepare ourselves to a certain extent. Thinking and talking about death need not be morbid. Ignorance and fear of death overshadow life, but knowing about and accept-ing death erases this shadow and makes life freer of tears and anxieties.

The fuller and richer the person's experience of life, the less death matters. The believer who is not afraid of death is not afraid of life. Such a person has confidence that God is in control, and that no matter what we may think about it, His will is going to be done.

2

Death-bed Experiences

There is a very important aspect of dying which has been known by hearsay for centuries, but which has only recently been made common knowledge by the advances of medical science in the resuscitation of those who have clinically died. This is that many people who are dying, or who actually did die briefly, are able to report back what they saw, felt and heard as they approached or passed the moment of death.

This is not a matter that should be hushed up, or relegated to the realm of cranks and fanatics – for the knowledge gleaned from these experiences is of enormous value and benefit both for the dying person and for those trying to come to terms with their death and mourning afterwards.

People who sit by the dying report frequent inexplicable changes in their dying patients or loved ones who regain temporary consciousness, changes which make them feel they have come back from another world with new and enriching experiences, or have learned something about themselves they never knew or were unable to express before.

Even people with the strongest of faiths are apprehensive about dying. If they are soon on their way to Paradise, how real is that Paradise? Is it anything more than a beautiful idea? What, honestly, would happen when they died? Did God Himself really exist at all, and would they see Him?

One test of any religion is how far it stands up to the crises of life, especially the final crisis of death. The shock of having to come to terms with death often makes believers examine again the whole basis of their faith.

Here are the words of some people who were on the very brink of death, but somehow, by the grace of God, did not die **but** returned to life and health.

'All pain vanished.'

'I went through this dark, black vacuum at great speed.'

'There was a feeling of utter peace and quiet, no fear at all.'

'I was in a very dark, deep valley. Later, I thought, "Well, now I know what the writer of the Psalms meant by the *valley of the shadow of death* (Psalm 23), because I've been there."'

'After I came back, I cried off and on for about a week because I had to live in this world after seeing that one.'

'It opened up a whole new world for me . . . I kept thinking, "There's so much that I've got to find out."'

'I heard a voice telling me what I had to do – go back – and I felt no fear.'

(*Life after Life*, R. Moody)

Research evidence

These are all statements taken from one of the many modern studies made by people interested in the whole business of 'healthy' dying. The medical profession has learned a great deal about the process of dying, but there are still many questions concerning the actual 'moment of passing' and the experiences people have when they are pronounced medically dead.

The evidence supports what has been taught ever since God revealed it to humanity – that there certainly *is* life after death. It is quite clear from the findings that most dying patients continue to have a conscious awareness of their environment even *after* being pronounced clinically dead! How can we possibly know this? Simply because nowadays, thanks to the improvements of health care, and various processes which can be used to 'bring back' a person even after they have clinically died – *the patients can themselves speak up and tell us so!*

Many people 'return' after death, thanks to electric shock treatment, heart massage, or the 'kiss of life'. In these cases, many reported the experience of 'floating' out of their physical bodies, associated with a great sense of peace and wholeness. Many were aware of the presence of another person who helped them in their transition to another plane of existence. Most were greeted by loved ones who had died before them, or by a religious figure who was significant in their life and who, naturally, coincided with their religious beliefs.

These facts have to be stated, since these experiences apply to people from *all* walks of life – Christian and non-Christian, and are not confined to any particular nation, culture, ethnic group, age range, or to any particular mode of dying. They are universal to human beings everywhere. Cross-cultural studies are now in progress, which are producing fascinating findings – although there will always be people who refuse to consider the evidence on the grounds that if a person 'came back' it could never be proved that that person had actually been 100% 'dead'.

No doubt, many members of religious institutions might be upset by the fact that research is now being done in such a taboo area as the awareness of people during and after the moment of their deaths – but since the research has now been under way for more than two decades, and there are now many thousands of recorded investigations, it is pointless and obtuse to bury one's head in the sand and try to ignore it.

Some scientists feel, for reasons best known to themselves, that this sort of investigation is 'unscientific'; some religious people feel that the question of life after death should remain an issue of blind faith, and not be questioned by anyone. Either way, no matter what their feelings, the research is going ahead.

However, genuine faith has always taught that the Truth stands clear from Error, and has nothing to fear from investigation. At no time does that statement become more moving than at the moment of death, when each individual stands alone and faces what must come.

The view held by Jews and Christians and Muslims alike has always been that some part of our selves survives death, even after the physical body has ceased to function, and is destroyed or decomposed. This persistent aspect has been called by many names – psyche, soul, spirit, self, being, and consciousness. Actual historical evidence for the belief goes right back to Neanderthal Man; religious evidence for it goes back to the earliest revelations to humanity, and underlies ALL theology

Muslims, for example, are taught not only that people have souls, but that it is perfectly possible for the soul to leave the body even before the moment of death. The Qur'an suggests in several places that souls may leave the body during sleep.

A ray of hope

It is He who takes your souls by night, and has knowledge of all that you did by day.' (Surah 6.60)

'Their limbs do forsake their beds of sleep, the while they call upon their Lord in fear and hope.' (Surah 32.16)

Some Christians are familiar with the child's prayer.

> 'Now I lay me down to sleep,
> I pray thee, Lord, my soul to keep.
> If I should die before I wake,
> I pray thee, Lord, my soul to take

It is certainly a fact that most people are not very happy about the prospect of dying, and thanks to the embarrassment of many of the living (who cannot face up to true loving care of the terminally ill) a lot of people die very lonely and unhappy deaths. This chapter should at least give everybody involved with the process of dying something to ponder, and may give an important ray of hope and joy to add to their faith. It is always the duty of the believer to add knowledge to faith.

As the modern world is now quite liberally sprinkled with living human beings who have at some stage actually been pronounced dead, but who have lived to tell the tale – it is surely foolish not to listen to their descriptions of what it is like, and try to learn from them.

As it happens, I have had the experience myself – or, at least, the next closest thing to it. I did not actually die, but I was very ill with a temperature of around 105 degrees. At this time, I was very unhappy, for various personal reasons. At around 9 o'clock one night, after being very ill all day, I suddenly found myself on a beautiful green hill, a very brilliant green, so bright that I thought to myself 'this is very strange, I have never seen bright grass like this before!' Although this experience happened to me about fifteen years ago, I can still remember these thoughts as if they were happening now.

While I pondered about this grass, I suddenly felt myself shoot forward and 'zoom in' until I was actually standing on the grass. Then I was overcome with the most surprising and wonderful sense of warmth and happiness and peace – it was the most blissful and delightful feeling, and so unexpected.

Next, I became aware that there was someone moving across the grass towards me. It appeared to be a young man, but I cannot remember his face or anything about him, except that he appeared to be overcome with joy to see me. Although I could not tell you who he was, I knew instinctively that it was someone who loved me very much, and that I deeply loved him, though not in a physical way. He was overwhelmed with thanks and happiness that at last I was able to return to him, after all this long time, and seemed to be drawing me towards him. Although I felt confused, I had the most strong urge to run to him, knowing that I had left behind all my sufferings at last, and could now find peace and joy back in the 'place' where I belonged, and amongst loved ones who deeply cared for me.

(The most hurtful thing to my children, when I told them later, was that I had not given *them* a moment's thought – I was so overwhelmed by this sense of welcome and joy. This was the one aspect I regretted telling my children, but it was the truth).

Suddenly, I felt as if I had been caught up in a whirlwind, and I was sucked away down a black tunnel, and came back to consciousness in my bed with an almighty thump. I cannot describe the devastation and disappointment I felt at discovering that I was still alive. I can remember the keen knife of that pain to this day; and if the whole business was a dream, I have certainly never had another experience like it, either before or since.

I would not have thought so much about this experience, were it not that so many others have had similar things happen to them, things which require an explanation.

Since that time, I have remarried and am now deeply in love with a very solid, human man, and have no desire at the moment to die and leave him behind, and go 'back' to anyone else. The mystery of death and what happens afterwards, and the secrets of our future relationships remains behind the veil for me.

All I can say is – I am *sure* that on that occasion I very nearly died, and if I had completed the process and 'gone', then no matter what symptoms my physical body down there on the bed were going through, my soul was blissfully happy, and perfectly content to go. I have never been afraid of death since.

This is my own personal testimony and it is very similar to those of people who have actually been declared clinically dead and later have been resuscitated.

Here is another example, this time concerning a lady friend of mine who 'died' in childbirth. She suddenly became aware that she was floating just near the ceiling, and when she turned and looked down, she saw her own vacated body lying on the bed, and the nurses dealing with her baby that had just been born. She knew the sex of the baby, and that it was perfectly all right. To her consternation, however, the medical team did not try to resuscitate her, but drew the sheet up over her head. This upset her, but before she had time to think what to do she found herself floating out of the room and along the corridor to the canteen where the night staff were having their cup of tea. There she could not make anybody see or hear her, but she could hear what they were saying. Then she felt sucked back, and fell down with an almighty thump, and sat up (still covered in the sheet) to the amazement of a young Christian nurse who was praying by her bedside! She was able to recount what she saw and heard in the canteen, and when the staff checked, it was found to be quite accurate. She was immensely excited by the experience, has never forgotten it, and is now no longer afraid to die – although she also now realises how quickly and without warning death can come to a person – so she values the lives of her loved ones more, and has become more tolerant of their small failings.

The subject of death is usually considered taboo. To be in contact with death confronts us with the prospect of our own deaths, draws our own time closer and makes it more real. Most people, after contact with a dead body, feel very uneasy (even medical students), because the thought inevitably enters their minds – 'That will happen to me, too.'

To spare ourselves this psychological trauma, we try to avoid the topic as much as possible. It is difficult to discuss death anyway, because the words of our language allude to things that we *have* experienced, and death lies beyond the conscious experience of all those who have not been through it. We end up talking in euphemistic analogies, which – if the real experiences of the dying are anything to go by – are totally wrong, and very unrealistic.

We are told that dying is like *going to sleep*. Or, it is said, it is *like forgetting*. When one dies, one forgets all one's woes; all one's painful and troubling memories are obliterated.

Others think that death is simply the annihilation of all conscious experience altogether, forever. If this is so, it has no desirable features whatsoever, since sleep brings rest and the possibility of renewal refreshed, and forgetting the painful memories brings relief at least. Annihilation implies that *everything*, pleasant as well as unpleasant, ceases to be.

All of these statements seems to be the very opposite of what 'dead' people report to be the case!

If God exists, Afterlife exists. The two are interlinked, and it is as simple, or as difficult, as that. For the religious person, death is not annihilation, but the passage of the soul into another dimension of reality.

The 'facts' can be studied from three groups of 'evidence' categories – people who have been resuscitated after having been thought or pronounced clinically dead by their doctors; people who, because of accidents or severe injury or illness, came very close to death; and the experiences of people who, as they were dying, told them to others who were present.

These experiences do not always fit in with what religious teachers and believers would like to think was the case. Let us take an example from one of the books of an eminent specialist in death-bed care, Dr Kubler-Ross. She was visiting the house of a little girl with terminal cancer who was pitifully ill and past the point where life seemed possible, and yet seemed unable somehow to find peace in death.

'During one of my house-calls I asked the little girl "Is there something that prevents you from letting go? You cannot die, and I cannot figure out what it is. Can you tell me?" With great relief the child confirmed this by saying, "Yes, I cannot die because I cannot go to Heaven." I was shocked by this statement and asked who had told her this. She related that she had been told many times by her religious teachers that "no one goes to Heaven unless they love God more than anyone else in the world". With her last physical strength she leaned forward, put her arms around my shoulders, and whispered apologetically – "You see, I love my Mummy and Daddy more than anyone else in the world."' (*Living with Death and Dying*, E. Kubler-Ross).

The role of the doctor was then not to react angrily to the stupidity of well-meaning people, but to convince the child that God did love her, very much; at last this poor child then she felt able to let go, and die.

Symptoms experienced

When people die, they experience very similar symptoms, although no two people are exactly the same. The most common symptoms recorded are these:

1. you hear someone pronounce you dead;
2. you feel yourself come out of your body, and may find yourself floating near the ceiling;
3. you can look down and see your own body, and watch what is going on, and observe any resuscitation attempts;
4. you hear a loud noise, ringing, or buzzing;
5. you feel yourself moving rapidly through either a tunnel of light or a dark tunnel with a bright light at the end of it;
6. you become aware that you have a soul. It is still like a 'body' but it is of a different nature from the one you have left behind;
7. on the 'other side' you see other people – perhaps dead relatives or friends that you recognise, or a loving warm spirit you have never encountered before, a being of light;
8. you are asked to consider your life, to evaluate it, and perhaps make some decision about it;
9. you may see a panoramic instantaneous playback of the incidents of your life;
10. you approach some kind of barrier or border, (a lake, a grey mist, a door, a fence, a window, a gate), and a decision is made about return;
11. you probably resist the idea of return, and do not want to

lose the feelings of intense joy, love and peace;

12. you fall back rapidly with a thump, often instantaneously, and find yourself back in your physical body, often with great pain;

13. you cannot find the words to describe your experience adequately;

14. you remember the extraordinary vividness of the experience for the rest of your life.

Researchers have not found any one person who has had *all* of these symptoms, (and there are some other fairly frequent symptoms not listed here), but many report at least twelve of them. The order varies; and people who were literally declared 'dead' got further along the chain of happenings than those who merely approached death. Some people recover from 'death' and remember nothing at all; others have the experience of dying more than once, and have 'nothing' on one occasion and the full series of events on the other.

The descriptions are inevitably very varied. Take, for example, the dark tunnel. Here are examples of how it has been described:

'I was moving through a weird dark place, it was like a sewer or something.'

'I went through this dark black vacuum at super-speed. You could compare it to a tunnel, I guess. I felt like I was riding on a roller-coaster train at an amusement park.'

'It was an utterly black, dark void. It is very difficult to explain, but I felt as if I were moving in a vacuum – it was like being in a cylinder which had no air in it.'

'A dark void – I stayed there for a long time just floating and tumbling through space . . . I was so taken up with this void that I didn't think about anything else.'

'A very deep, dark valley. The darkness was so deep and impenetrable that I could see absolutely nothing, but this was the most wonderful, worry-free experience you could imagine.'

'I entered head-first into a narrow and very dark passageway. I seemed to just fit inside it. I began to slide down.'

'I found myself in a tunnel of concentric circles. Shortly after that I saw a TV programme called the Time Tunnel . . . well, that's the closest thing that I can think of.'

Surprise

When people 'come back to life' after these experiences, their chief reaction to what they have been through is one of surprise. Most of the time people identify with their physical bodies, and do not take the point of view that they are really souls inhabiting temporary bodies, even though their religion may have taught them that. It is often only the experience of 'tasting' death that brings it home to them (and the persons involved with them).

Many people find the notion of existing out of their bodies so extraordinary that when they experience it they are totally confused, and do not necessarily link it with the idea that they are dying for quite some time. They wonder what is happening to them, why they can suddenly see themselves from a distance, as though a spectator.

Emotional reactions vary wildly. Most people report, at first, a desperate desire to get back into their bodies, but they do not know what to do. They recall that they felt very afraid, even panicky, especially if they saw the medical people covering their bodies up with a sheet and wheeling them off.

The dying person's feelings of loneliness are soon dispelled, however, as they get deeper into the experience. At some point, others come to give aid in the transition – reported as taking the form of deceased relatives or friends, or in a great number of instances, a spiritual 'being of light'. Individuals who see this being report that it has the most profound effect upon them. Typically, when it first appears, it is a dim light which rapidly gets brighter until it reaches unearthly brilliance – usually said to be 'white' or 'clear' or 'like lightning' – and yet it does not in any way hurt the eyes or dazzle them, or keep them from seeing other things around them. Virtually all the people interviewed expressed no doubt whatsoever that it was a 'being', a being of light, and it had a definite personality of love and warmth which emanated to the dying person.

This feeling of bliss is utterly beyond words, and the dying person feels completely surrounded by it and taken up in it, completely accepted; they sense an irresistible attraction to this light.

What is interesting is that people of different faiths interpret this being in different ways – some Christians state that it was Jesus, Buddhists and Hindus see a figure that fits in with their religion, atheists see a 'shining person', Jews and Muslims report 'an angel'. By this they do not mean a figure with wings or a harp, or even that the being had a human shape or appearance – what comes across is that the being is a *guide*, someone sent.

Since we have no evidence whatsoever as to the form the angel will take, it is quite reasonable to suppose that people of different religions will see the angel in a form which appropriates to their own particular cultural expectations. To assume (as some Christians do) that the angelic figure is none other than the Blessed Jesus himself may be no more than the result of simple piety, and a rather naive allocation of a very onerous and mundane role to one of the greatest of beings – although this is not to say that our Lord and personal saviour might not be so loving and kind as to attend personally the traumatic moment of passing of his loved ones. Who knows?

Make them think

The communication which follows is not with words, but with instantaneous understanding, and often takes the form of questions: 'Are you prepared to die?' 'Are you ready to die?' 'What have you done with your life?' 'What have you done that is sufficient?'

All those who have had this experience insist that the being is not there to condemn them – it does not accuse or threaten, for they all feel total love and acceptance coming from the light, no matter what their answer may be. The point seems to be not to pass judgement or to condemn, but to make them think about their lives.

Then, in a moment of startling intensity, the being presents to the person a panoramic review of his or her life. Some said these memories came instantaneously, everything appearing at once, and that they could take it all in one mental glance. Yet it is incredibly vivid and real. Even if quite a few of the things they have done are wrong, or even evil (as they inevitably are, for there is no such thing as a perfect person), and they have cause to feel ashamed, the 'being of light' does not condemn, merely opens their eyes to see how they can learn from this review.

Here is one death-bed experience remarkably like my own:

'I "died" from cardiac arrest, and as I did, I suddenly found myself in a rolling field. It was beautiful, and everything was an intense green – a colour unlike anything on earth. There was light – beautiful uplifting light – all around me. I looked ahead of me, across the field, and I saw a fence. I started moving towards the fence, and I saw a man on the other side of it, moving towards me as if to meet me. I wanted to reach him but found myself being drawn back, irresistibly. As I did, I saw him, too, turn around and go back in the other direction, away from the fence.'

(Life after Life, R. Moody, p. 73–74)

Obviously, all the people in the reported case studies had 'come back' from death, otherwise we would not have their information. In every case interesting changes had taken place in their attitude by this time – once the dying person reaches a certain depth in the experience, he or she does not want to come back and may even resist the return to the body. This is especially so for those who have gone so far as to encounter the being of light.

Here is another case history, which gives much food for thought:

'I was with my elderly aunt during her last illness. I helped take care of her, and all that time everybody in the family was praying for her to regain her health. She stopped breathing several times, but they brought her back. Finally, one day she looked at me and she said, "Joan, I have been over there, over to the beyond, and it is beautiful there. I want to stay, but I can't stay as long as you keep praying for me to stay with you. Your prayers are holding me over here. Please don't pray any more." We did all stop, and shortly after that she died.'

(Life after Life, p.81)

A similar case was reported of the famous Jewish Rabbi Joshua shortly after the time of Jesus. As he lay dying, his disciples gathered in the room next door, which was both their synagogue and their school. Here they prayed hour after hour for his recovery. He couldn't die. Finally, a pious maid went in and stopped the disciples at their prayers 'For what are you praying? You are praying for his agony. He is with God, let him be!' He died, and the Talmud praised her for this action.

(*Jewish reflections on Death*, J. Riemer, p.125)

It must be emphasized that however you interpret these experiences, a person who has been through it has no doubt whatsoever as to its reality and its importance. The people are quite capable of distinguishing dream and fantasy from reality, and are functional, well-balanced personalities. Often – and this is of vital importance – their attitude to the rest of their life on earth changes completely. They are more 'at peace', more reconciled, regard their remaining days or years as 'precious', and virtually all stress the importance in this life of trying to cultivate love for others.

They don't feel morally perfected, or 'holier-than-thou' – but have new goals, new insight, and a new determination to live in accordance with their new goals and understanding.

Incidentally, none of these experiences bear much resemblance to the Paradise or Hell they had been taught to expect from their religious training, (except, perhaps, the 'beautiful gardens', parks or grass), presumably because the experiences of the souls immediately after death are quite different from the ultimate fates to come when souls are reunited with bodies on the Day of Resurrection; there seems to be no evidence or indication of reincarnation.

Suicide, as an attempt to escape the stresses of this life, was pointless – if you leave here a tormented soul, you are still a tormented soul 'over there'. (In fact, attempted suicides reported that in their disembodied state they were unable to do anything about their problems, and they also had to view the unfortunate consequences which resulted from their acts!)

Research has largely concluded that these death-bed experiences are not caused by hallucinatory drugs or medicines taken near death (the experiences people who have when they are confused by drugs are very unclear and muddled!), or anaesthetics, or lack of oxygen. People who *are* drugged or anaesthetized do also report experiences, but their cases are quite different – the 'visions' are confused rather than perceived with great clarity, there is no personified brilliant light, or ineffable feelings of peace and happiness; and such 'visions' as they do have *are* created largely out of their religious cultural expectations – they *do* talk of heaven and hell and angels, and 'going up' and golden gates, and so on.

Christians should take much encouragement from the comfort and excitement these cases bring to the living, and rest assured that the experiences seem to be in keeping with the teachings of Christianity, even if some of the points raised are rather surprising to people who have never considered the nature of the soul's condition in the afterlife, but have simply assumed that it would 'sleep'.

The important thing is that there is a great responsibility on the people who are attending the dying, not to interfere through drugs, thoughtlessness or impatience with what may be the person's most important experience, and may give meaning to their dying.

Not only that, but paying attention to dying people's observations are of tremendous importance to the outcome of the mourning process of those left behind, and may well change the attitude of the bereaved to their own future deaths. To faith add knowledge.

If it can be demonstrated that the process of death is nothing to fear and that our souls are often released from suffering bodies even before that body draws its last breath, and that they painlessly and with great joy enter a new and active state, then death has lost its sting. Hospital staff, or any people with no belief in life after death, have no right to attempt to deprive either the dying persons or their relatives of this experience.

3

Grief Reactions

If we lose someone close to us, such as a spouse or child, we immediately feel helpless and lost, like we did as infants. When a beloved husband or wife dies, or a child loses a parent, the key figure on whom the mourner had based the content of their life and security has gone. No matter how strong the faith of the mourner, those remaining behind are left unhappy and frightened, feeling they have lost part of themselves. Without strong faith, the despair and sense of chaos may be profound.

Here is part of a 'letter' one mourner wrote to her mother, who had died suddenly. This person had been very close to her mother, and could not face the prospect of continuing life without her:

'Mum, I'm sitting here crying, the pain is so intense I am so afraid of cracking up. You have been the main thing in my life all these years, how can I let you go? What is there left for me now? I am going to break into a thousand bits and vanish into the black sea of pain and loneliness.'

Awareness

This is the desperate cry of someone who does not have the patient faith in God that brings inner serenity. Look again at the words – they are certainly heartfelt, and full of agony. But two things are obvious, firstly that the person is concentrating on 'I' and secondly that there is no awareness of God. She says – 'You (her mother) have been the main thing in my life'. If she had made loving her mother her first concern, because of her love for God, then the mother's death would be seen in perspective, and it would not be so painful for this person to let her go.

She grieves: '*I* am crying, *I* am in pain, *I* am cracking up, *I* can't let you go, nothing is left for *me*, *I* am going to lose *myself* and vanish!' In fact, all her thoughts are concentrated on herself, and her anger and bewilderment with her mother for leaving her. The grief is all for her own predicament. This is perfectly normal and natural, but quite untouched by faith. With faith, the natural sorrow for the passing away of a loved parent is transmuted by the expectation that they have not ceased to be, but have gone to stand before God, to receive forgiveness of their sins, perhaps the reward for the toils and efforts of their completed earthly tests, and certainly the gift of God's grace – the loving welcome into His nearer presence.

Some people come out of grief strengthened; others become strained, depressed, anxiety-ridden, or develop psychosomatic symptoms. Only one thing is for sure – everyone who has been affected by grief can never be the same again. Some people find healing forces in their grief, but others end up as clients of the social and health services.

Shock is the first response to the death of someone who has been important to us, and that shock is particularly pronounced when it is a sudden unexpected death. It may find expression in physical collapse, in violent outbursts, or in dazed withdrawal, denial, and inability to take in the reality of what has happened.

Mourners often complain that they were not prepared for what it would be like – 'Why did nobody warn me that I would feel so sick ... or tired ... or exhausted? Or that grief felt so like fear?' In fact, grief is one of those things that cannot be taught by the book, but which only makes sense after the experience.

Because bereavement is so upsetting, and the symptoms so traumatic, it may comfort mourners enormously to know that certain symptoms and feelings are almost universal responses to grief and loss, and that every mourner is not only entitled to have and express these feelings, but also that it would be wrong and perhaps harmful for them to try to suppress them. If they love God, God will open their hearts and comfort them *even while they are in their grief*.

People in shock are often numbed and apathetic. Rest and warmth are the best methods of treatment – yet so often the bereaved are encouraged to 'keep going ' and 'get busy' , as if the important thing was to put the grief right out of their minds. This is no remedy, but could actually be harmful if it sets the scene for denial of loss and pain. People who 'hurry' the mourners into getting busy are probably only expressing their own fear of becoming involved in the mourner's pain.

Four tasks to help work through grief

There are four tasks which all mourners have to complete in order to be able to work through their grief so that they may in due course reinvest their energy in new life and relationships – the loss has to be **recognised**, the various emotions of grief have to be **released**, new skills have to be **developed**, and the emotional energy has to be **channelled** into newness of life.

There are four main phases of mourning. In the first state a bereaved person is numb and does not feel able to bear or accept the loss. This often leads to a kind of mental blockage, a denying that the loss has occurred at all, interrupted by outbursts of anger and/or distress. Denial can sometimes take the form of manic activity – either clinging on to every memory and belonging of the deceased, or the opposite, flushing out every possible trace of them.

A real advantage of a powerful faith is that this sense of numbness and denial can be sharply reduced, if the believer does not view the death of the loved one as a 'loss', but remains confident that the loved one has NOT ceased to exist but has gone to an afterlife prepared in advance for them.

'In my Father's house are many mansions; if it were not so, would I have told you that I go to prepare a place for you? . . . I will come again and take you to myself, that where I am there you may be also.' (John 14. 2–3).

Real Christians try to make a genuine effort to face death in confidence. They should be comforted if they are able to accept that they have spent all their lives trying to please God and living in accordance with His wishes as they understood them. They should also be confident that the Lord will have mercy on any of their weaknesses and failures, so long as they lived according to a good intention and were penitent for any recognised wrongdoing.

Usually the phase of acute shock lasts only a few days.

Shortly after death comes the next phase, in which practical arrangements have to be made and the funeral faced and endured. In this period, the mourner is usually surrounded and supported by relatives and friends.

The presence and sympathy of others, and the 'special' position in which the mourners find themselves, do to a certain extent give them a sense of 'safety'. Christians need not feel that they have to be guilty about their grief, or that this shows a failure of their faith. Even if they have believed in life after death from their youth, their sorrow is understood and they are expected to give vent to their grief, and to need support. Those with good support may literally feel that the others will see to it that things do not get out of control, that life will go on.

The real pain and misery make themselves felt when this controlled period, and the 'privileges' that went with it, are over, and the task of coming to terms with the new reality begins. It is then that the mourner can really feel lost and abandoned, and try to build up defences against the agonies of pain.

Searching

The second universal phase in mourning, which usually starts after the friends and relatives have withdrawn and the bereaved is trying to cope again, is that of yearning and searching for the lost person. They weep and 'call' for the deceased loved one. This 'searching for the lost one' is an almost automatic universal defence against accepting the reality of the loss. It may go on for a long time.

Quite frequently, things happen that convince the mourner that the soul of the departed one is definitely still around Sometimes the bereaved 'see' the lost person in the street or around the house; they 'see' them in unguarded moments, at the end of the bed, or in dreams. They often 'feel' lost spouses beside them in the bed; they smell the drift of familiar perfume, or of tobacco.

Many mourners visit the grave frequently, or go to places where they spent time together with the dead loved one, feeling that by doing this they are coming close to them again. While in this phase, the mourner is frequently very restless, unable to concentrate, and insomnia is very common. Sometimes, there may be outbursts of anger or distress. The mourner may not be aware of the 'need' to search, and may indeed deny this as a nonsense – but it is there, nevertheless, expressed in their restless behaviour, tension, and loss of interest in all that does not concern the deceased.

The person who believes all these 'symptoms' to be no more than the longings of an unhappy bereaved person has no right at all to insist upon this point of view. Some people have a very powerful belief that their loved one is still with them, consoling them, and not wishing to be parted from them, and despite the scepticism of the non-believers, there is no proof that this is not so. This powerful belief is shared by religious and non-religious persons alike.

However, there is one word of warning which must in all sincerity be given to the bereaved. Whatever our fate in the life after death, it cannot be a good thing for the departed soul to remain 'earthbound', forever tied to the people and places they should now have left behind (unless this happens to be God's will). This is one reason why the faith of a believer is so important, in letting the 'dead' loved one go.

Try to see it from the point of view of the 'dead' person. If it is true that they can see the awful grief and distress of those they have left behind, it will inevitably cause great pain and distress to them, especially if they *cannot* get these loved ones to see that they are 'all right' and not suffering any more. It must be quite heartbreaking for a 'dead' mother or spouse to watch the distress and break-down of their loved ones, and not be able to do anything about it. Certainly, they would be very reluctant to move on, and leave them in this state.

I feel quite sure that this is one reason why God allows so many bereaved people to have a glimpse of their 'dead' loved ones – whatever the cause of the phenomenon – and perhaps pick up the sensation that 'all is well now'. It enables them to be comforted by the thought that they are no longer suffering, and are in 'God's hands', whole and happy; and so the survivor can let go.

These symptoms lessen bit by bit as the bereaved person slowly accepts the reality of loss – but it is doubtful if the impulse to search ever completely disappears when the lost one is dearly loved.

Faith comes to the aid of the grieving soul. Christians regard the state of the departed souls as a mystery known only to God; if it is His will for that departed loved one to be felt or seen by the griever as a comforting presence, then it is God's will – and no one will be able to deny this close feeling. Many people feel very aware of the good wishes of their dear departed, consoling them. The mourner is then able to take courage, and to recognise that the departed one is NOT lost, but safe on the next stage of their journey.

Since the awareness of afterlife is so strongly felt in these cases, the pain of grief is transmuted from one of irrevocable loss to the lesser pangs of being parted only for a while.

Acceptance

The third phase encountered in mourning is the heartbreaking agony of disorganisation and despair. This is probably the most painful part of the experience for a non-believer, when the bereaved person begins slowly to change from protest to resignation, and finally is forced to accept that the loss is irreversible. The dead loved one is never going to return, and no matter how much they might like to leave this earth and 'go with them', it is not God's will, and they must start life afresh without that person.

This acceptance can only happen when the bereaved person feels strong enough to bear this knowledge. In fact, the denial, pretence and numbing of feeling that characterise the first phase are necessary defences against pain that cannot yet be borne.

The Christian encounters all these natural feelings just the same as a non-believer, and tries to cope with them. It is, of course, quite devastating when a loved one passes on, but the true Christian knows in the heart that it is a duty to accept whatever will God has for their lives, even if they cannot understand the reason for their suffering and loss. They know that all humans are mortal, and the times of their deaths were known by the omniscient God from the moment they were conceived. They can draw consolation from the knowledge that the 'dead' person is not really dead at all, but is in another place, experiencing other things; and that how they react to that person's loss is a very real part of their test of life.

If God wills, the loss of someone we love will not be final at all, but there will come a time when we are re-united. Until that time, we should try to bear the pain patiently, and not let our grief become a cause of concern for the 'dead' loved one.

It may well be that although the time may seem very long to us, for the 'dead' loved ones who have gone outside Time as we know it, it will pass in a flash.

Believers should take comfort in regarding their own lives as gifts from God. It is the highest act of faith to be prepared to give this life back to Him without argument, resistance or complaint; to give it eagerly, when called for. If a Christian lives every day in the service of God, to their best ability, then it is not so difficult to accept God's call when it comes, and reply humbly – 'I am ready. At Your command, O Lord.'

One beautiful example of this submission concerns the wife of the famous Jewish Rabbi Meir, who had to break to her husband the news of the death of their two sons. She said to him – 'Many years ago a stranger passed this way and left in my safe-keeping two precious jewels. He has been gone so long that I have come to feel that these jewels are now my own. Now today, unexpectedly, he came back and demanded that I give him back what is his. Must I, indeed, give them up?' Rabbi Meir said to her, 'How can you doubt the right thing to do?' She took him by the hand to the other room, threw back the sheet, and said, 'There lie the jewels.'

(From *Jewish Reflections on Death*, J.Riemer, p. 132)

Face up to life again

The last phase of mourning comes a long time later, when the bereaved really can relinquish the lost person, and begin to face up to and adapt to everyday life again, without that person, and without a compulsive clinging on to every little memory. Only after the mourner has lived with the loss and, perhaps, built up the beginnings of a new life, is it possible to accept the finality of the loss.

All too frequently the grieving person develops symptoms that are treated with tranquillisers and anti-depressants, but this is only a covering up of the pains that are hurting, a temporary relief – and one, moreover, that may be building up more problems for the future if the 'patient' becomes dependant on those drugs.

In order to recover from the loss it is necessary to go through each of the four stages outlined above, to strengthen one's faith and hope, and not to regard mourning as an illness, or anything to be ashamed of. Mourning is not an illness at all – it is the cure to the grief.

Probably the most vital and useful part of that mourning is the faith of the bereaved person. It is their faith which gives them the patience to bear the loss, to accept God's will gracefully and with resignation, to pass through their time of mourning with dignity and true acknowledgement of reality, and to turn their eyes forward to new life with hopes unshaken.

4

Giving Help to the Grief-Stricken

How can one be of help to the person who is in mourning?
The kind of help really needed is what is known as 'crisis and
grief therapy', a process of help designed to mobilise the
mourner's healthy forces when the grief process is being
blocked or is so difficult that the process is turning pathological. If the bereaved person is a Christian of good faith, then
the task is made that much easier, because certain factors will
be taken for granted. Nevertheless, human beings are human,
and the pains of a spouse grieving for a lost partner, or a
parent for a lost child, or child for a lost parent, are
excruciating.

*It is no help whatsoever to 'nag' the grieving person, or
adopt a sanctimonious attitude – one which 'reminds' them of
their great faith in God and the afterlife and reproaches them
if their faith seems to be wavering or if – in the opinion of the
'helper' – their grief seems wrong because it seems to deny
their genuine belief and trust in God.*

You cannot force a person to stop grieving, any more than
you can force a person to fall in love, or believe in God in the
first place. It is worse than misguided when an over-pious
person actually adds to the mourner's grief and pain by harping
on their apparent weakness, and reprimands them – usually
from the stance of moral superiority.

Our dear Lord understands the mourner's loss perfectly well
– when his beloved friend Lazarus died and was buried, Jesus
did not assume an off-putting superior stance as a result of his
great faith and knowledge. He wept.

'When Jesus saw (Mary) weeping, and the Jews who came
with her also weeping, he was deeply moved in spirit, and

troubled, and he said "Where have you laid him?" They said to him, "Lord, come and see." Jesus wept. So the Jews said, "See how he loved him!"' (John 11. 33–36).

How can we help mourners? Only by remembering our Lord's gracious promise and believing it.

'Martha said to Jesus, "Lord, if you had been here, my brother would not have died. And even now I know that whatever you ask from God, God will give you." Jesus said to her, "Your brother will rise again." Martha said to him, "I know that he will rise again in the resurrection at the Last Day." Jesus said to her, "I am the resurrection and the life he who believes in me, though he die, yet shall he live, and whoever lives and believes in me shall never die."'(John 11. 21–26).

Consolation

This is the most wonderful consolation, and bringer of hope. Even when we are so bowed down that we do not know how to cope or carry on, God is with us – on the darkest night, in the deepest despair. He knows our suffering, and will be with us through all our period of panic. If we stand firm, confident of that love and those promises, then our pains will not destroy us.

Crisis help is the giving of emotional 'first aid' when the loss or the traumatic experience is so overwhelming that the grievers are in danger of being submerged by their emotions.

The most basic help of all is to realise that every mourner should have somebody to stand alongside them, so that they do not feel alone. Help can be quite simple, and physical – a hot drink, a blanket, an affectionate arm or hand; little touches like these make all the difference in the world.

The most valuable healing ability for any human being, is the ability to shed tears, so it is therefore very valuable if the bereaved person is able to give way to this expression of sorrow. if the mourner is 'bottled up' or 'pressed down', the crisis-helper might perhaps choose a suitable moment to say something that will release these healing floods which bring relief to the soul.

There is an old story which gives a mythological origin for the tear:

'When Adam and Eve were driven out of the Garden of Eden, God saw that they repented of their transgression. He felt pity for them, and gently said: "Poor children! You are entering a world of grief and unhappiness that defies description. But you shall know that I am generous and that my love for you will last for ever. I know that you will encounter much adversity and that it will embitter your lives. Therefore I bestow upon you my most precious treasure, this costly pearl – the tear. When you are overwhelmed by grief, when your hearts are about to break and great pain is clutching your soul, then this tear will fall from your eyes, and the burden will at once be easier to bear."'

'Calling Weeping'

The first sort of weeping done by the grieving person is known as the 'calling weeping'. At this stage, the mourner is still resisting reality and trying to hold on to the lost person. 'Calling weeping' involves shallow, rapid breathing and does not bring the same relief as the deep weeping which occurs when the bereaved person mentally lets go of the deceased.

Weeping is important, because in the tears are forces that heal both physically and mentally. Tears have a relieving effect on the stress produced by loss and trauma. It really is a gift from God – humans are the only animals that react to stress In this way.

It is therefore useful to remember that it is harmful when growing children are told that weeping is weak, or childish, or that things are 'nothing to cry about'. The person's ability to grieve could be impaired, and therefore the adult later might be unable to resolve the stresses in a natural and wholesome way. Some children gradually learn to control themselves so well that as adults they never weep. Others can be tearful, but without giving way to deep releasing weeping.

The weeping that heals is the profound sobbing in which the tensions of the body are let go. The tensions arise from the muscles of the body contracting as a defence against both physical and mental pain, so that the pain does not become too overwhelming for the body's autonomic nervous system. It may also unleash chronic tensions which derive from any old unprocessed traumas lingering from the past. Tears probably also restore the body's natural balance in connection with stress. Investigations show that the chemical content of the tears in weeping is different from that of the tears from eyes that are 'watering'.

How do you help a weeping person? Should you ignore them, or try to stop them, or encourage them to 'let it all flow'? When a person is weeping, some appreciate body contact and others do not. The befriender could try putting arms around the mourner – it is a simple matter, and you can easily judge whether it is appreciated or not. Some people are comforted by this, others stiffen and become insecure. If in doubt, ask if they wish it. Sometimes it is precisely this body contact of a friend that gives the necessary courage to 'let go'.

How does the mourner feel? They feel overwhelmed by pain, tears, guilt feelings, anger and fear. They have difficulty in sleeping, their hearts palpitate, they suffer indigestion, stomach disorders, body aches – in fact, their whole nervous system has been disturbed.

These mourning symptoms are not just confined to people who have lost a dear one. Obviously, when people grieve it is because they have lost someone or something to which they were closely attached, and people can be attached to a multiplicity of things – human beings, money, job, prestige, home, land and other possessions. Appearance and health are two other powerful 'attachments' – if someone loses a breast or an arm, leg, or eye, or becomes badly disfigured by disease or fire, then they understand the great importance of this attachment. All these losses trigger off mourning symptoms, and need 'healing'.

Psychologically, people who have previously had difficulties in their attachment process towards other people also have problems in living through the emotions of grief in a healing way. When facing bereavement, all the past memories of loss, grief and abandonment come to the surface again, and old wounds – even memories from childhood – are re-opened.

If something has happened in the past for which grief was never completed, the new occasion for grief can open the floodgates that dammed up the past trauma too, and healing for both can take place. Grief always needs to be healed – many times grief in adulthood can heal suppressed griefs from childhood days.

Normal grief Stages

Research has shown that normal grief follows three main phases: (a) deliverance from the past by recognising the significance of the loss in all its facets; (b) rebuilding the present with a new everyday life that contains both what is left and some necessary changes; (c) the experience of having a future with new possibilities.

Grief is not a disease, but if incorrectly handled it can easily develop into one. It is not in itself sinful, but if clung on to it blocks the healing powers of faith, and room is given for the devil to take over. Suffering can sometimes be a powerful motivator towards insight and goodness but if wrongly handled it can also alter people's characters in sinister and life-destroying ways. It is quite possible to die of a 'broken heart' and sober factual research shows clearly that mortality increases by an enormous percent in widows and widowers.

We have to accept that the loss is a reality, that our sick loved one, who has perhaps been ill for a long time, is dead. Every day some 200,000 people die – by disease, mischance, murder, starvation, war, natural catastrophe. Some die whilst still in the womb, others from old age. Some die at peace with the world, others fighting all the way.

The bereaved person must face up to the recognition that their loss is irrevocable. This is sometimes achieved quite easily then the beloved one has been 'released' after a long and painful illness, but it can be more difficult to accept in cases of 'sudden or violent death.

If the deceased was loved, respected and cherished, it takes a long time to sink in that they have gone for ever from this earth – that perhaps for years the mourner will never again see the loved one, hear the well-known voice, feel their loving arms or kiss. A bereaved partner has to accept that they no longer have a future together.

The death may mean that we have to live without bodily warmth and sexuality. We may become half a couple. At first, the pain will grow, because the recognition that the loss is irrevocable will slowly become plainer. The mourner will have to change his/her life, and learn new skills, and ask for help in different ways from before. Only eventually will the mourner learn to invest energy in new ways, which shows they are reconciled to their grief.

5

Letting Go

Some people, especially men, suppress their grief – they feel that they must not let it show, not in front of the children, or in front of their religious friends. It is important to them that life must go on, that they show their faith to be genuine – as if God anywhere required us not to grieve for our loved ones! If they are suppressing their grief, these people will become restless, even hyperactive. They are not getting rid of the problem, merely putting it aside for a while. Months or years later a sad film, or sympathetic shoulder, or anything, will trigger off and reopen all this suppressed grief, and they will be obliged to face it after all.

If grief is not fully expressed and worked through, all sorts of psychosomatic symptoms occur – vague pains for which an organic cause cannot be found; actual ailments like peptic ulcers, heart conditions, asthma, headaches etc. Sometimes the bereaved develop symptoms that closely resemble those of the deceased.

There are psychological symptoms too – sadness, emptiness, anxiety, vehement self-reproach, guilt. Some develop a strong dependence on others, or alternatively a total isolation and cutting off. They display phobic behaviour towards things that belonged to the deceased – either stripping the house of reminders, or keeping a bedroom as a shrine.

Healthy grief is flexible, pathological grief is more rigid. It is normal to leave the deceased's bedroom untouched for a while after death. But what then? Does it become a shrine of memories, everything remaining untouched forever as a memorial room? Is there complete avoidance of the room? Is everything got rid of so that no reminders are left to disturb the mourner? If everything has to go, that may betray an emotional rigidity which may inhibit work of grieving – the mourner is foolishly trying to live as though nothing has happened.

In some bereaved people, thoughts about the dead person and emotions of grief replace almost everything else and go on for months if not years. These grievers almost worship everything that had to do with their loved one. Bedrooms remain untouched for years, the clothes worn by the deceased are kept hanging in the wardrobe. Sometimes a bereaved person keeps the clothes, but does everything to avoid the room associated with the lost one. Sometimes they isolate themselves so much they become bitter and unapproachable.

Controversy rages over whether it is better for relatives to see the corpse or not. In some cultures it is normal for the relatives of the deceased to take upon themselves the task of rendering the final washings and swathings of the body, and not to leave it to strangers. The last intimate services to the loved one are done with care and respect. This is itself an aid towards healing grief.

Seeing the body

Seeing the body of the deceased is an important part of the mourning process. The encounter with the stiff lifeless form makes it easier to recognise that they are gone, and to let them go. The sight of the corpse is usually quite enough to trigger off the healing reaction of grief naturally. It makes it clear beyond doubt or false hope that the farewell is inevitable.

If the body of the dead person has never been seen, as in a case of loss at sea, or in a bombing – it is very difficult to accept. Maybe the missing person is still alive somewhere? The mourners cling desperately to their forlorn hopes.

The sight of the corpse usually triggers the recognition that their spirit has gone forever – the body is no more than an empty shell. The loss strikes home, the controls come down, and the bereaved person begins to weep. This viewing of the corpse is therefore not just a morbid curiosity it is very important. Some people argue that they wish to keep in their minds the picture of their loved ones as they were, and not the sight of their dead corpses. However, it does seem that if the dead person is not seen, the parting is that much more difficult.

There is a human need to say a final farewell, and most people feel cheated if they are deprived of this. Children should not be excluded from this farewell, either, and their grief should be taken just as seriously as that of the adults. Caring mourners should prepare children for what they will see, and perhaps hold their hands through the farewells.

Adults who lost parents as children feel cheated if they did not see them and make final farewell. Mothers should see their stillborn babies. If they see and bury their dead babies they are well started on their work of grieving.

After a death, many people have the need to recount over and over again the details of that death. Now, the helper is most valuable not for speaking, or 'finding the right, words', but just for being there, and for taking the time to listen patiently.

If the reality of their loss is not accepted, it may be that crisis intervention is needed. The mourners will probably not take kindly to it, for they are beset by a massive denial of reality. Their reaction tends to be – 'You mustn't say that – it's too cruel!' The person helping them through their grief has the task of making them face up to their loss.

The bereaved person is possibly full of despair, fear, feelings of being abandoned, loneliness, perhaps guilt and shame. Other common reactions are violent anger – against the world, against fate, against God or against the deceased. The person's soul has been shaken. You will often hear them say things like: 'How could he die and leave me?' 'I can't live without him.' 'Everything worth living for has gone.'

It is pointless trying to convince the mourner that these statements are a nonsense – it is how they feel and that feeling is strong and real. The true facing of reality has to come later, and in Christianity it is made so very much easier by the acceptance of God's will and the sure knowledge that when we die we deliver our souls into His keeping.

Sometimes it can be useful to use a simple metaphor to help the mourner to widen their perspective on their pain. You could tell them they have a choice. They can be a chick or an egg. If they choose to be an egg, then they'll see the end of their relationship with their dead loved one as the destruction of the whole fabric of their life. It will split in half and fall into

two empty halves. Alternatively, they can see themselves as the chick that comes out of the egg. In that case they will feel small, very vulnerable, greatly in need of warmth and comfort and food. Above all, they'll have the craving for security. But as a chick they will grow. A smashed eggshell never recovers.
(Adapted from *Men and divorce*, J. Abulafia, p. 102.)

An understanding friend

Often the bereaved person needs someone with whom they can think aloud, and who is there while they work out their own solutions. A friend on the end of a telephone may provide just the sounding board which can enable us to face and articulate fears which might otherwise take hold of us. A friend who is willing to make a *regular* commitment to a bereaved person is doubly valuable – they are not only helpful, but their regular help provides much-needed stability in this uneasy time. Someone who can 'be around' for as long as the bereaved person has need of them, is a real life-line.

The unhelpful response is to jump to conclusions and be over-anxious to protect. We can be very good at giving unwanted advice, and complicating simple issues. The helpful response is to be still, and to accept, enabling the person to go at their own pace. Anything more than that divests the mourner of what dignity they have left, of their ability to make their own choices, to be a growing person.

Helpers must be calm, strong and sympathetic, able to understand and empathise, a fixture of security and authority. To approach the grief-stricken person with too 'matter-of-fact' a manner is just as bad as being too sugary. A true helper can weep with the mourner, but should not have their broad view blocked – they should try to show how there are healing forces to be found in the tears and anger of the mourners, so they should not be afraid or ashamed of them. They can help to reduce fear, shame and guilt by convincing mourners that their grief is a healthy sign, and not an illness.

Some mourners develop bitterness and chronic grief and withdraw into isolation, convinced that nobody can really understand how difficult things are for them. The bereaved may feel so impoverished that they become deeply depressed and feel they cannot continue to live. They may not even want to live, because only life with the dead loved one had any value. Mothers or fathers who have lost idealised partners may so instill in their children the feeling that everything worth having belongs to the dead that they burden them with constant self-doubts. This living with death is the very opposite from accepting death.

There are many factors which influence responses to bereavement, such as mode of death (how did the person die?), timeliness, previous warning, and preparation for bereavement; but the key factors seems to be genuine faith, and the relationships or interactions that existed between the surviving and the dead.

The loss through death of a person who was important to the one left behind strikes at the deepest roots of human existence, recalls the experience of previous attachments and losses, and reactivates the pain of earlier bereavements, physical as well as psychological.

Emotionally deprived and threatened children sometimes try to avoid the fear of abandonment and isolation by denying their feelings and pain. If they do this, they suppress healing reactions and postpone feeling the agony of the final bereavement through death. If life does not later help them resolve the anxieties which underlie these defences, they may go on to repress and deny other feelings – including the positive ones of love and joy as well as sorrow – and develop into unfeeling, unemotional people.

Feeling of loneliness

Loneliness is one of most poignant forms of human suffering. It is a desperate feeling of separation from those who give meaning to life. The loneliness that accompanies acute grief is an assault on the meaning of life itself. It is an acute threat to the inner security system of an individual. It is the devastating loss of some of the essential nature of the self.

When people truly love others they become vulnerable. When they are so concerned about another that whatever happens to them also happens to themselves, they extend the perimeters of their capacity to suffer the happiness is shared, their injury is felt. When a loved person is devastated by death, the part of yourself you invested in another has been temporarily lost; the bereaved person is longing for the part given in love to another.

There is a perverse satisfaction in wallowing in the misery of loss and separation. Someone may misinterpret their feelings in such a way that they glorify grief and try to hold on to it as a proof of their love and willingness to suffer as a result of it. These negative responses cripple life and reduce it to partial existence, and are against the spirit of faith.

When we recognise this loneliness and emptiness for what it is, we relieve to some extent the misgiving we may have about it. It is nothing to fear or be ashamed of. It is a fact of life that verities the fact of love. But our life does not end with the death of another, and likewise our capacity to love does not end with the loss of the object of our love. The capacity for love remains waiting for a chance to express itself anew in ways that can continue to enrich life. This is not disloyal.

'Perhaps one of the deepest needs of those who confront the distress of acute grief is to be kind to themselves. And it is certainly not being kind to oneself to entangle one's life in a mass of fantasies and vehicles of self-deception. Nor is it useful to assume that one is so strong that one never needs help; for there are times in life when all of us can benefit from the strength, guidance, and wisdom of others whose perspective has not been clouded by the stress of acute grief.'

(*The many faces of grief*, E. Jackson, p. 56)

Recovery from the wound of grief has been compared to recovery from a physical wound. Physicians can alleviate the pain and support the natural healing powers of physical wounds, but for the wound caused by the loss of a loved person every mourner needs special sympathy and support from the people around them.

Only when the lost person has been 'internalised' and become part of the bereaved, a part which can be integrated with their own personality and enrich it, is the mourning process complete, and adjustment to a new life can be made. Then the dependence on the external presence diminishes and the bereaved becomes able to draw on memories, happy or unhappy, making it possible to talk, think or feel about the dead person.

'Letting go'

The final stage of mourning comes when the bereaved can calmly accept the loss of their loved ones, and turn to face renewed life without them. It is a time when they have often to acquire new skills household management, cookery, driving a car, financial paperwork etc. Although a painful time, it is also a time for personal growth possibilities and a new independence. It often brings a closer relationship with new other people.

The final farewell for a bereaved person comes when they can say goodbye to all their joint hopes, dreams and earthly plans and ambitions. Their thoughts and feelings have to slowly let go of the dead one, for the wound left has to heal before that person can be whole again, with the dead person as a fond memory in the heart. It does *not* mean, of course, that the bereaved person has to say farewell to all memories of the loved one.

This 'letting go' is a natural process which cannot be speeded up by anyone's help or by therapy. It takes a normal person from 9–12 months before they can begin to take their energy from the deceased, and some 2–3 years before they are ready for new relationships. Many people live on without letting go of the deceased for the rest of their lives; this may be acceptable, but they should be aware that if they have to face fresh losses, all the old grief will be opened up again.

6

Anger and Guilt

One aspect of the distress of bereavement is that neither the love for the lost person nor the mourners themselves are perfect – as a consequence the bereaved often experience some self-hate, self-accusation and guilt.

Their anger and hostility may take quite irrational forms. It can be directed against the medical people who looked after the deceased, the nearest and dearest, and the dead people themselves – the lost ones who have caused the bereaved one so much distress by abandoning them!

There is also a great deal of suffering caused by guilt – guilt about what was said or not said, done or not done, justified guilt and guilt with no rational justification. The guilt may be the result of realistic regrets about insufficient care and concern, or it may be based on fantasy. In fact, our guilt is often a mixture.

Some mourners feel very guilty because they believe they failed their loved ones on their deathbeds. They intended to stay with them while they died, but when it came to it could not face it and fled the room; or perhaps they left the room briefly for some perfectly justifiable reason, and it was during those few moments that the loved one died. We dwell on what we might have done differently; and this indicates that we have not yet abandoned the mental hope that the death is irreversible.

'I went away, I went and left you, Mum'. 'I was weak, frightened, couldn't bear it – so I left you alone.'

Mourners may feel guilty for not having told their dying ones of impending death, and thus depriving them of any preparation for it; for neglecting them, not loving them enough, not giving them enough strength. Maybe they became impatient or distressed, and wished that the dying ones would die quickly, and 'get it over with'.

Devoted mourners may suffer excruciating guilt for very

trivial reasons – if only they had not argued yesterday, if only they had sent the wife to the doctors earlier, or to a different doctor! Some feel guilty because they feel they should be grieving more, or differently. Usually they are criticising themselves quite unreasonably – a kind helper can ask them to describe all the things they actually did. This helps to restore perspective.

When a loved one dies, we will *always* be able to find something we wish we had done differently, something to blame ourselves for. We are human beings, not robots, and human beings *do* fail. If we demand perfection of ourselves and our relationship with the patient we shall probably give far less than if we can relax and accept that if everyone does the best they can, that is sufficient, and no failure is final – with God.

God not only forgives our failures, He sees our successes where no one else does, not even we ourselves. Only God can give us credit for the angry words we did not speak, temptations we resisted, patience and gentleness little noticed and long forgotten by those around us. Such good deeds are never wasted nor forgotten, because God gives them a measure of eternity. All the wrong we have ever done can be forgiven and forgotten if we are willing to bring it to God. It is never too late to find peace with God, or to make peace with those we have wronged.

Release from guilt

It is important for mourners to be released from unnecessary burdens of guilt. Maybe you could suggest that they take the opportunity to return in their imagination to the death-bed and do something different. Confront it again, and this time, be able to say farewell. If you believe in the afterlife of your loved one, then this is not a silly thing to do – the loved one will understand perfectly all that you *intended* to do.

Don't feel guilty! Don't forget, often mourners are already in a state of shock when the death of their loved one occurs. If you like, you can talk to that departed one as if they were still there, able to hear you. Tell them everything you wanted to say – that you love them and wanted to say goodbye. Weep and sob like helpless child, and do not feel ashamed. Then *feel* the loss which you were keeping at bay.

At a later stage, some mourners find themselves feeling guilty when they begin to recapture the sense of joy and growth. They feel they are 'letting down' the dead one by abandoning their deep mourning. This is a terrible and tragic mistake. They are not letting the dead loved one down at all; just because someone you love has died *does not mean that they have stopped loving you* – and if they are aware of your too-great grief and unable to do anything to console you, it would cause them pain. Try to think of it that way round. Your dead loved one would *wish* you to pick yourself up, and be able to enjoy the rest of your life. Your dead loved one would not wish you to become helpless, or ill, or bitter, or paralysed emotionally.

In the same connection, it is quite wrong for other people to add to the struggles of mourners by deliberately trying to make them feel guilty if they are beginning to come out of their grief. Instead, they should be helping them back to life!

Sometimes, when a mourner *has* behaved very badly to the deceased, they find relief for their guilt by devoting their lives to paying restitution. Someone who was 'hated' during their lifetime suddenly becomes cherished, a 'saint', very special, very important, someone who never did any wrong. What is happening is that the mourner is idealising the deceased – the false claims of the deceased's 'saintliness' are really attempts on the pact of guilty mourners at restitution, a defence against the pain of their guilt.

Most mourners, out of respect for the dead, idealise their deceased to a certain extent, which may reinforce the denial of real feeling and the memory of a real relationship. The dead person suddenly becomes 'too good to be true'. A useful question to help bring the mourner back to reality is – 'what *don't* you miss about that person?'

A recognition of the universality of this need to idealise may help any mourner who shows exaggerated responses. If they can be made to see that most mourners go through this stage, than maybe they will start to forgive themselves, and accept reality. If they can then be helped to see the lost ones not only with all the loved and admired aspects of their personalities but also with the irritating and feared ones, the 'warts and all', then the exaggerated mourning and idealisation may become modified, and the bereaved may become able to see that they still loved them, even in spite of their faults!

Many of the anger feelings are quite natural. The mourner is thinking – 'How could you desert me with all these problems, children, etc?' 'Why didn't you go to the doctor before?' 'Why didn't you take more care of yourself, stop smoking, etc?' 'I could kill you for the pain/mess you've caused me.' 'God, how could you let an innocent child die?' 'Why am I being punished like this?'

'Ask any grieving person directly if they are angry with the deceased, they will automatically deny it and say 'no'. It is not done to speak ill of the dead. Sometimes mourners are very shocked and afraid of this sudden upsurge of anger in themselves, and it adds to their guilt. They think they *shouldn't* be thinking like this. It seems very disrespectful of the dead. Once again, if they can be brought to realise that this is also a natural part of their mourning, and almost universal, they will be less afraid of their emotions and forgive themselves in due course. Once again, a kind helper could ask gently what it is the bereaved miss about their lost ones; then ask what they do NOT miss a few times.

There is one serious danger in anger. Often, in times of great stress such as coping with death, people may be afraid of letting their anger explode outward, so they turn it against themselves, bringing about the result of clinical depression. Sometimes they even believe that they *cannot* go on without the lost one, and contemplate suicide. This may actually be a way of saying 'I am so angry at myself that I must punish myself!' The self has laid upon itself the 'duty' of being its own executioner.

When anger becomes intolerable to the individual, the consequences may be serious indeed. Anger has to be admitted, analysed, acted out and abandoned – and the hardest thing is probably admitting it. We must lift it up to objective examination. Why am I so upset? Does my behaviour or attitude make sense? The kind helper encourages the mourner to back off and look at the anger – realise where it comes from. It can be a weak spot in personality – it is not worth what it causes in inner stress or fractured human relationships. If possible, it should be abandoned for insight, understanding and healthy action.

To be able to feel guilt is not bad, but a gift of God. It is a sign of our capacity to *feel with others*. If we do something that hurts them, we can feel the hurt. Throughout the years as we grow towards adulthood there is a build-up of this capacity, and this is healthy and important. Our whole system of law and order is founded on the assumption that human beings are creatures capable of feeling guilt, and that guilt usually keeps them from injuring others or violating their rights.

There are at least three different kinds of guilt involved with bereavement. There is real guilt, where somebody really has done something to regret, and the cause-and-effect relationships are obvious. In these cases, the mourner really has let the deceased down in some way, and they know it. They cannot turn the clock back and put it right, so they suffer guilt as the inevitable result.

Secondly, there is neurotic guilt. This is where the guilt effect is out of all proportion to the cause, and its origin is largely in the tormented mind of the bereaved person. The mourner is feeling much more of the painful emotion than is warranted by the circumstances. There is an impulse here to self-punishment.

Thirdly, there is existential guilt, which is so deeply implanted in life that cause-and-effect seem to be irrelevant – this guilt is felt because an individual is trapped in a generally poor opinion of his or her capacities, not because of any particular act or event. We can see an example of neurotic guilt when somebody who can ill afford it insists on burying a relative with a very expensive or ornate gravestone, or organises costly 'funeral parties' or 'remembrance services'. It is too late to make amends to the deceased directly, so the guilty party does the next best thing and punishes the wallet, and thereby discharges the personal obligation. It is as if they were openly pleading guilty of neglect and asking for a fine.

Religious people suffer in certain specific ways that do not bother those without faith. The most difficult and painful of all the suffering to which a religious person has to adjust is that of reconciling the real and *actual* state of their heart and emotions with the standards they have mentally set for themselves as a result of their faith. In other words, many religious people know very well what their attitude of faith is *supposed to be*, but find they are suffering just as much as the non-religious person in actual fact – in which case, their suffering is increased by the burden of guilt at their 'lack of faith'.

Sometimes, of course, the cause *is* lack of faith – but quite often this particular guilt is a neurotic one brought about by a wrong understanding of faith, or of the nature of God.

Let us take one simple example – the burden of 'keeping up appearances'. This is quite a severe task, especially for a man trying to maintain those emotions and feelings he has been brought up to believe are 'manly' and right. There is a common fallacious belief that men are only fully masculine when they perform roles that show them to be active, in pursuit of definable goals. A truly masculine man is most at home in the external world of action. He pays a price for this mis-belief, for when he finds himself confronted by the internal world of thought and emotion, he feels lost, ill at ease, on 'foreign ground'. The deeper he is drawn in to his emotions, the more he feels his masculinity is endangered.

Such men can suffer dreadful agonies of hurt and remorse when a wife or child dies, because they regard women and children as weaker than themselves, and feel that they have 'failed' in their protection of those in their care. If a wife or child dies, some men go further, and angrily accuse God of failing *them*; neither they nor God were able to protect their loved ones.

Need for wider viewpoint

This is neurosis, and not religion. If you think about it, it is a way of challenging and complaining about the will of God – who knew from the moment of the conception of that loved one in the womb the exact moment when their souls would leave their bodies. There is no point whatsoever in fretting about this – the decision concerning the length of one's time-span here is always fixed and known by God, no matter how much it may catch us humans by surprise. We are not given to know the reasons why certain things happen in our lives, or the time-schedules for them.

Sometimes we get very upset by what happens, but then, we should sit down and try to raise our thoughts to a higher level, in which we see from a wider viewpoint that if God takes away a loved one it is for a reason, and our test is *not* to see if we can continue to grieve and think about nothing else but our loss for the rest of our own lives. This is *not* disloyalty to the dead loved one, but acceptance of a higher plan.

One common reason behind a man's attitude of anger when he loses his wife or children is associated with possession. Many men have an enormous problem seeing their wives or children as separate individuals, and regard them virtually as their possessions. This again is wrong, and a man with this attitude should try to alter it.

However, the reaction of anger is accepted by many men, and understood – because anger and desire for revenge are 'manly'; grief is not merely thought to be 'womanly' but also an abdication of responsibility. To 'give way' to tears and grief is to suffer a loss of masculinity. Some masculine men actually feel fear if they let themselves 'give in' to grief. They think that if they do this they will be overwhelmed, paralysed, emasculated, unable to keep control.

These fears and assumptions are not based on a rational, thought-out response to the world as it is. They are not being logical – but it is no use asking why a man should feel less masculine if he cries; the fact is, he does, and will try to stop crying as soon as he can. He will try to 'master' his emotions.

This, too, is wrong, and they should not feel guilty if they cannot stop their weeping. Their tears are not a sign of their 'failure', or of God's 'failure', but of genuine love and sorrow at the temporary parting. They are not a sign of weakness at all, but of depth of love. Christians should never blame God for 'failing' them – if something happens which they do not like or understand, it is their duty to accept it as a test, and make the best reaction to it in patience and humility. As it happens, anger has quite an important function in the mourning process of many people. If they have gone numb inside and shut out all their emotions, it is anger which often breaks through the numbness and denial, and so frees the person who was locked up inside their own loss.

The price men pay for being 'protective citadels' is that it becomes 'risky' for them to admit having vulnerable emotions like fear, grief, sense of failure, longing for something or a man's deepest assumptions about who he is, his maleness, what makes him valuable. The most effective way he sometimes finds of dealing with the problem is simply to pretend and convince himself that it doesn't exist.

Denial, however, is only a short-term method of coping with trauma. If a person has suffered physical injury, the body sometimes copes by denying pain that is too excruciating to bear – it goes into *shock*. Sometimes a badly injured person does not feel pain for quite a long time. Shock is the body's first line of defence.

But eventually the pain returns, and it has a specific function – it indicates the place and nature of the injury. If we didn't have the pain, we wouldn't know how to set about the process of mending the injury. Emotional trauma is very similar – the person who has lost a partner, child, (or things like home or job), needs just as much ease and protection as if they'd been knocked down by a car. They need peace, calm and attention, so that their healing process can begin.

If the badly injured person insists on limping off, asserting that nothing is wrong, you'd say he was in shock and that this deception wouldn't last. Sometimes, after death, people suppress and deny their grief symptoms, and force this to become their way of life, thinking perhaps that everyone around them and the society in which they live will applaud this way of behaving, and think that the best way of dealing with their 'injury' is to forget it for good.

This behaviour is actually not brave, nor commendable; it is stupid. You cannot lead life as usual if you have a broken leg. Nor can you lead life as usual with a broken heart. The real problem for all injured people is getting better, and you can only do this if you allow the injury to heal. This can only begin to happen after you acknowledge that you have been hurt.

7

Fear and Forgiveness

It is human to be afraid, and nothing to be guilty about. It has nothing to do with sin or doing wrong. Fear is a feeling, a sign that we are alive. Without it we are probably suffering from a physical or mental handicap. It is a signal that danger is near. We need to feel fear. If we refuse to notice fears, we begin to allow them to dictate how we behave. We will not be in control, but will be possessed and driven by our fears. This will lead us to become confused and divided inside, and go on to produce forms of anger and violence.

Unacknowledged fear is dangerous, and like nuclear waste, it cannot be disposed of; it can only be stored. It goes on acting and developing in destructive ways. Facing fears means facing facts, and facing the truth can be uncomfortable, but it does slowly release the grip of fear. We have to face the truth in order to stop pretending, deceiving ourselves and other people.

Acknowledging fear is not easy, especially if we condemn it in others or regard it as a sign of failure in ourselves. 'Big boys don't cry', 'Christians should not be afraid'. We receive this impression in youth and grow up believing it to be true.

But big boys do cry and Christians are afraid. Yes, maybe the ideal is someone who is self-sufficient, independent, reliable, mature – no weaknesses; but we should not forget that even Jesus cried over Lazarus, and was afraid of death in Gethsemane.

Much suffering can be caused by believing that Christians should not be afraid. If we cry and feel fear, we are not failing we are simply being human. What matters to the Christian is how we react to our fear, how we tackle it. Acknowledging fears becomes easier when we begin to realise that certain fears are universal to all human beings – so we can hardly be blamed for having these fears. Once we can realise that we are not special or different, stop expecting ourselves to be 'super-human'. Let us be honest – keeping up the pretence of freedom from fear is exhausting and inwardly painful, like having somebody stick pins in our legs under the table while we have to pretend all is well, and not show anything on our faces.

We have so many fears – fear of failing people's expectations; fear of losing dignity by admitting we need help; fear of criticism and disapproval, and of losing our reputation. When we develop fear of losing control, or of involvement with others, we begin to isolate ourselves. We develop an island mentality, and surround ourselves with a sea of loneliness.

We put up the façade of independence, and begin to believe in our own pretence. Because of our pride, we begin to believe that we are self-sufficient, and become increasingly unable to acknowledge what we can and do receive from others.

This self-inflicted isolation causes us to appear aloof or shy, and people begin to believe that we do not want to be approached at all and so our loneliness and fear of losing control increases all the more.

Sharing our fears with anyone is risky – we risk rejection. Our listener may judge us and desert us, and in our wounded state we dread being cut off and excluded. It takes real determination to find someone to trust and confide in. Making friends is an adventure and takes courage. It is dangerous because it involves trust, openness and love, and if trust is betrayed then openness turns to cynicism, and love can turn into hatred and rejection. The fear of betrayal, cynicism and rejection often prevents us from even attempting the art of friendship, so we allow ourselves to be caught in this wretched cycle of fear. In effect, we create our own isolation and deny any possibility of being comforted, healed or helped by a friend.

Opportunity to grieve

For the Christian the tragedy of a person's death is not the end of the story. Christians have confidence that there is life after death. Therefore it seems to many Christians quite illogical to grieve the loss of someone who has simply left this earth and gone on to other things. This is theoretically true, but even while believing in the life to come, it is still unhealthy to skip too quickly over the feelings of loss and tragedy that bereaved people experience.

We *shall* feel a sense of loss, and an aching void, if we have been close to the person who has died. We need to acknowledge those feelings in ourselves and in other people. It is part of acknowledging the whole truth.

This is one reason why funerals are so important – they are times when we give each other the opportunity to grieve and also to express our faith in God and the future life. Death can then be transformed, very gently, from tragedy to triumph.

If we do not talk about our fear of death we deprive not only ourselves but also our children of a healthy facing of reality. They will grow up unprepared for loss. It is more helpful when there is no pretence or camouflage. Losing precious things does hurt. Facing death is about facing loss. We have to learn how to regard our bodies as 'God's', and be prepared to give them back when He wants them.

Once we have found the courage to confront our fears, and share them with another person, we begin to feel more alive. The paralysis that has gripped us gradually lets go and life returns. We begin to face the future with new energy.

Fear of death stalks us until we accept that this is part of what it means to be alive. We need to discover how to live the short span that we have to the fullest extent. This only really becomes fully possible after we have been 'touched' by death.

It is not wrong to be human. We need people to accept us just as we are – confused angry and hurt. It is because of our inability to accept one another that we become afraid – we fear judgement and punishment.

Many images of God portray him as a stern unmerciful judge only concerned with condemnation. This makes us feel throughout our lives that we are in the dock, fearfully awaiting our sentence. Yet Christians know in their hearts that this is only a partial picture of God's nature – He is both righteous and merciful, and knows all there is to know about suffering.

Dominant parents, teachers and other authority figures in our childhood reinforce our picture of the stern judgement of God, and if we were brought up by over-restrictive adults we may have developed into unbalanced, fear-driven human beings who expect rejection at every turn, and who feel safe only when relating to a rule book of behaviour. We go on to reject ourselves and condemn ourselves and each other, by banishing the bits we would rather not own as if they did not exist. This contributes to a destructive way of life where we damage not only ourselves but others as well.

Dealing with our feelings

It is damaging to deny disturbing feelings; it is how we confront them and deal with them that matters. Feeling angry with someone is not wrong, but nursing that anger in private becomes destructive. Accidentally falling in love with someone else's wife is not wrong, but nurturing that feeling leads to irresponsible actions which break up another person's life.

It goes without saying that the aim of all Christians is to live in such a way that they should be free of fear. If their lives and actions are acceptable to God, and they genuinely accept that their lives are no more than His 'gift' and must be relinquished into His hand when He requires, then there is nothing to fear in death. But it is wrong for someone to point the accusing finger and maintain that any signs of fear appearing are signs of weakness, and try to make Christians feel guilty for 'letting God down'.

God knows that we are human. Our fears are not signs of disobedience or sin which need to be punished, but human frailties which need understanding and compassion. Christians who feel that they have to apologise for being afraid, often go on to believe that they are not good enough, and God will not accept them. This craving for perfection is actually unhealthy and damaging – and challenges the will of God who was pleased to create us human. Learning to accept ourselves as God accepts us is a very difficult lesson for some! It seems incredible that God should find us acceptable, loved even, just as we are, with all our imperfections – so long as our intention is in accordance with God's will.

Sometimes religious people develop a neurotic guilt which leads to a very peculiar 'cosmic fantasy' – they believe that God is deliberately manoeuvring painful events in order to punish them for their misdeeds. It is quite common to hear people gasp 'Why did God do this to me?' This attitude distorts the basic structure of the universe in a way that makes a person doubly vulnerable to the crises of life. At a time when a friendly cosmic force is most needed, God may become an enemy!

Although painful events may well occur as the result of our sinfulness, cruelty, selfishness or neglect, the fate of one person is NOT a means of punishing another. No human being can pass through this life without hurt or loss. No person is immune to biological bacteria, or the laws of gravity, etc. We live in a world of natural laws, of cause and effect, and sadly – no matter how much we might fantasize and wish it were so – if someone fires a bullet at our head, it is unlikely that God will miraculously intervene and catch the bullet.

Some very pious Christians seem to find it impossible to believe that God is like the father in the parable of the Prodigal Son. He sees all our failings and weaknesses, and still loves us. He waits only for us to turn to Him and express our sorrow at our inadequacies – and He forgives us. Punishment is not the fate of weak mortals who are sorry, but those so hardened by their lives of sin that they *refuse* to repent. Sending someone to Hell is never of God's choosing, always the fault of the one who denies.

Sometimes those who have always been 'righteous' get very annoyed with God for His generous benevolence towards the penitent weak ones; they cannot bear the thought of sinners 'cheating' their deserved punishment – but this is not what Jesus taught in the parable of the Prodigal Son, or the Labourers in the Vineyard.

Many Christians are confused about what is acceptable to God. They have allowed themselves to believe mistakenly that Christianity is primarily about good behaviour. Yet behaviour is about what we do and not about how we feel. Jesus knew anger and fear just like the rest of us, and went on to show that we have the resources to handle our feelings like that without doing wrong.

God knew we would not be perfect, and that we would hurt one another. He knew that there are ways of changing our behaviour to be more loving rather than less loving; to be more accepting rather than less so, and to be more creative and less destructive. But He left us to choose which way we want to go. Jesus did not moralise or repeat multitudes of commandments – he lived a certain way. He showed us the kind of life that God would like us to follow.

He showed us that God loves and accepts us as He made us, and stays with us through suffering, even through deliberate wrong-doing or sin, helping us to learn to practise forgiveness and to change our ways, becoming more loving human beings.

When Christians rush to judge themselves, or each other, then they lose the possibility of loving, replacing it with feelings of guilt and fear. The world outside is deterred by the apparent double standards of those within when they preach love and acceptance on the one hand, but practise judgement on the other. The people criticised most by Jesus were the hypocrites. He exhorted people to face the truth about themselves, and see the faults in themselves before they rushed to judge others.

With God there is no ulterior motive, no strings attached. He loves us with a pure love that has no wish to dominate, manipulate, or coerce. There is no compulsion in His pure love. He loves, He waits, and leaves us to respond when we are ready – and He goes on loving, whatever our response.

Unconditional love, or grace, is not like an anaesthetic, imposing a false sense that pain has ceased. It helps us *in* our infirmities, *while* we are suffering, *during* the times of great fear, to face what is happening. Grace comes to help in time of need.

When we harden our hearts it is often because we have been hurt or felt threatened. When someone we care for dies or leaves us, it hurts, so we steel ourselves against it happening or hurting again. After a while, the grace of time helps us to take courage to risk ourselves again, in another relationship. But if we feel hurt or betrayed by someone who is still close to us, who is either dying or has died, we have the choice either to harden our hearts or to forgive.

Peace through forgiveness

Choosing to forgive is vital for wholeness. It makes all the difference to whether we blossom and flourish, growing healthy and loving, or whether we grow into bitter, withered and twisted people who gradually lose the capacity for living a full and rewarding life. The hurt we felt will turn to anger, and we will begin to hurt other people in return, contributing to a destructive way of life.

Being forgiven is part of the same process, and just as difficult. If we are aware only of *forgiving*, it implies that we can never hurt people and have no reason to receive forgiving ourselves. This makes us patronising and aloof, unaware of what holds us together. If the person we have hurt has died, then we have to confess our failings to God and allow Him to forgive us, and forgive ourselves!

Nothing is more pathetic than the person who runs out of life before he is dead. 'Forgiveness of others releases us and gives us peace – which is a prime factor in any healing. But there are also times when forgiving others is not enough we also have to forgive ourselves – and we sometimes find that even harder to do. We give lip-service to the fact that God freely forgives all our wrong if we confess it and ask for his forgiveness, but we do not let go of the guilt. We keep it like a stick to beat ourselves with, because unconditional forgiveness seems too much like an easy option.'

(*Face to face with Cancer*, M. Stroud, p. 149)

As Christians, we are not permitted to nurse a sense of guilt; we must fully and completely accept and embrace His forgiveness and love. Guilt feelings and inferiority before God are expressions of selfishness or self-centredness; by clinging on to them we give greater importance to our little sinful self than to His immense and never-ending love. We must surrender our guilt and inferiority to Him; His goodness is greater than our badness.

The peace that comes through this forgiveness brings healing and acceptance to the bereaved, and it is very important. There are persons who shape their lives by the fear of death, and persons who shape their lives by the joy of life. The former live dying, the latter die living.

'Where can we find the strength to master our fears, to achieve wholeness? There is a place. It is where we can all go before our health begins to fail more seriously. It is very near, and is the place where we can tell each other about our fears of growing old, of losing our loved ones, of losing our health. It is the place where we can talk about being afraid of running into debt, of hitting our children or of harming ourselves. It is the place where we can share together that we fear losing the power to love, to have children, or to be successful. It is a place where we bring our hurts, and find acceptance and love, and where we are enabled to feel better, and glad to be alive. It is a place where we do not feel ashamed of our fears, and where we can find courage to take action, knowing we shall not be alone. This place is the Throne of Grace. It is where God is, and is a place of prayer.'

(*An aspect of fear*, Grace Sheppard, p. 110)

8

Special Types of Losses

There are certain modes and circumstances of death that
require additional understanding – losses from suicide, sudden
death, sudden infant death, miscarriage and stillbirth, abortion
and anticipated death. These can all create distinct problems
for the bereaved, especially in families where suicide and
abortion bring particular disgrace.

(a) *Suicide*

Christians believe that every soul and life has been created by
God, and just as it is a great sin to kill any person unlawfully,
so it is equally wrong to kill oneself.

People who commit suicide are in a terrible state of stress;
they have lost faith and patience with life. When they are
being realistic, people understand that no human being can
expect to pass his or her entire lifetime without hardships and
sufferings, and when these come they should be faced up to
with courage and fortitude. The confident Christian knows
that God gives His peace in the midst of the storm but He does
not usually stop the storm on our behalf. when people are
brought to a state of desperation by something, it is often only
their faith in God that keeps them going. No one can deny
what a blessing it is to feel that no matter what happens
'underneath are the everlasting arms'.

Many old-fashioned Christian hymns express that comfort
and inner peace that comes from firm faith

> 'We have an anchor that keeps the soul
> steadfast and sure while the billows roll;
> fastened to a rock which cannot move,
> grounded firm and sure in the Saviour's love.'

In times past it used to be suggested that suicides had lost faith and were wicked people who would go to hell, and sometimes a hurt and aggrieved mourner will comment on this. It must be stated that there is no reference in the Bible of any such thing. Jesus gave no word on the subject. Sometimes the suicide's 'cry for help' is just as much a cry to *God* for help as it is a cry to other human beings.

As regards hell, it is obvious that the soul of the suicide will indeed be grievously tormented by the full awareness of knowing what he or she has done to the loved ones left behind; this is not the same thing as being consigned to a place of eternal punishment. Those bereaved by a suicide should try to remember that if it is true that there is life after death, then any person attempting to escape from their stress and problems by taking their own life will not succeed – because *they continue to exist*. Not only that, but in expanded consciousness they will now experience even more stress, for they can now see the terrible aftermath of their desperate action, the agonies of hurt and despair they have caused.

The suicide no doubt bitterly regrets doing it, but there is no way they can stop the hurt they have caused; they cannot go back, and they have to come to terms with that awful awareness. It can help heal a bereaved person who has fallen into the state of mind of 'why did he/she do this to me?' to think about it from the suicide's new vantage point and what they must be going through, and to find peace in healing and forgiving prayer.

Obviously, if a person has real faith in life after death, suicide can never be presented as an escape, and this is one reason why education regarding the out-of-the-body soul-experiences of those approaching death and the religious teachings about life after death are so important in a practical sense.

The minds of people who commit or attempt suicide are always zoned in upon their own painful situation. The two most common thoughts uppermost are either 'How can I stop, or get out of this painful situation?' or 'All this is *your* fault, and you'll be sorry now that I've killed myself!' Frequently, of course, the suicide did not really intend to end their life at all, and hoped to be saved at the last moment; they were really only intending to 'punish' their loved ones, or making a dramatic gesture as a cry for help.

Either way, they are feeling so desperate that it is a very sad situation. If a believer actually follows through and deliberately commits suicide, it *can* be regarded as a sinful act because not only is it in defiance of the will of God, it is extremely unpleasant for those left behind and a deliberate cruelty to them. (Incidentally, it is the return of responsibility, the thought of what will happen to those left behind, that has stayed the hand of many potential suicides. It is worth remembering that so many people who kill themselves got into the state when they believed that nobody cared about them, and their death would not matter. If only we could love our families more, and let them really know that they *do* matter!)

For the bereaved, there is not only the sense of loss, but also a legacy of shame, fear, rejection, anger and guilt. The suicide has sentenced the survivors to deal with the horror of the persistent thought that it was all their fault – they may not have tried hard enough, or they may have said or done something just before the suicide that they felt had triggered it off. They feel they may have either caused the suicide, or, at least, failed to stop it.

Suicide is the most difficult bereavement crisis for any family to face. Not only has the suicide 'failed' in life, but the family has also 'failed' and let the suicide down, by being unable to prevent them, cure them, or give them hope. This shame can dramatically affect the interactions of the bereaved with each other and with society. The same is true whether the suicide is complete or only attempted.

Some families cope for years with a potential suicide whose frequent (if unspoken) refrain is. 'If you say or do that to me, I will kill myself and you'll be sorry then.' What is happening here is that the suicide is subconsciously trying to foist the blame for the action of their own freewill on to others, and thus avoiding taking responsibility for their own life. Bereaved people suffering agonies of guilt because they 'slipped up' and said or did the wrong thing shortly prior to a suicide must be made to realise that they are *not* to blame for it, at all. The suicide's mental state is such that they would probably play the same game with whoever was looking after them, even a stranger.

The second major emotion is guilt – the bereaved often take

responsibility for the action of the deceased and have a strong feeling that there must have been *something* they should or could have done to prevent the death. This guilt feeling is particularly powerful when there actually was some conflict between the deceased and the bereaved.

Sometimes the guilt is felt so strongly that the bereaved do not ever really recover from the loss, but punish themselves in various ways, or begin to act in such a way that society punishes them – adults break down or become recluses, or turn to drugs and alcohol. Children frequently become delinquent, and suicidal in their turn.

The bereaved also feel intense anger. Not only are they angry about the waste of the life of the loved one, with all its potential and unknown future, but perhaps they are also angry because a great deal of their effort *had* gone into trying to help that person, all to no avail. They might also perceive the death as a personal rejection – 'How could he/she do this, after all we've done for him/her?' This rage then goes on to fuel their guilt feelings, because of its intensity. It is not uncommon to hear the bereaved state that if the deceased had not killed himself/herself they felt like killing them themselves, for what they had put them through!

Every person goes through traumas and challenges in life and normally they manage to survive without contemplating suicide. People who have come through suffering to a more tranquil existence later are frequently angry, frustrated and aggrieved by the attitude of the one who has 'packed it all in' and given up. Older people, who have been knocked about by life and recovered to enjoy pleasant experiences they would not have dreamt of during their unhappy times, feel particularly angry and frustrated that young people committing suicide could not think this out for themselves.

Along with the anger comes low self-esteem; the bereaved parent, spouse or fiance cannot help feeling that they were not good enough; they have been rejected. They assume (usually quite wrongly) that the suicide could not have thought enough of them, that their help and support must have been inadequate, or that the suicide might even have been trying to escape from them and could see no other way of doing it. They had preferred to die rather than talk things through with them.

When they sit and think about it calmly, later, it is helpful for the bereaved to remember all the evidences that the suicide did, in fact, love them very much. It was the suicide who had the overwhelming sense of failure.

The traumatic sense of failure in the bereaved needs urgent healing, for it can even lead to self-destructive impulses in them too; if they cannot throw off this trauma they spend their future lives carrying a sense of doom. It is an awful truth that suicide can sometimes 'run in families', the bereaved in one instance becoming potential suicides themselves later.

Apart from the usual bereavement therapy, in these cases the bereaved need curing of any distorted thinking, and they need consoling with particularly generous sympathy. They should gently be made to understand that the urge to commit suicide generally builds up over a long period, perhaps with numerous scenes, threats, bluff-calling and failed attempts. The suicide's family has probably been coping with a great deal of stress and depression for some time, usually drawing on reserves of love and patience way over and above the normal call of duty. That the suicide was not ultimately prevented is not the fault or responsibility of the grieved family.

Sometimes they try to find a way out of their guilt by seeing the victim's behaviour not as a suicide but as an accidental death, and a myth is created that disguises what really happened, thus avoiding the necessary stage of facing up to reality.

Much of the guilt is unrealistic, and making the bereaved face up to reality can bring enormous relief. Sometimes, of course, the guilt is real because the bereaved *were* in some way responsible for the suicide's feelings of failure, and in these cases they need help to deal with these feelings if they ace not to punish themselves consciously or subconsciously for the rest of their lives. They have to be allowed to see that everyone makes mistakes, has rows, says things they do not really mean, and that God really does forgive, so long as they honestly face up to their faults and are genuinely sorry.

It can bring great relief to the bereaved to talk to the soul of the suicide, and believe in their hearts that the suicide is aware of their thoughts, and that they can forgive each other. Then, they have to be encouraged to have faith in God by accepting the comfort that if He can forgive them, then they should put the burden down, and forgive themselves.

It is common for the bereaved to fantasize about the characters of suicides, either regarding them as having been all good or all bad – neither of which is reality. Those who create an idealised character for the deceased (and consequently suffer all the more deep guilt for their death) have to be made to see that this is not reality; in fact, their 'ideal loved one' was probably a considerable trial and worry to others, and was quite likely suffering from deep clinical depression, saw no way out, and in desperation took his or her own life. Once the bereaved can realise that the suicide was the victim of a clinical state which was not in any way their fault, they can relieve themselves of a large burden of guilt.

It is also helpful to realise that shame, guilt, anger and fear are all quite normal stages to go through – the bereaved can observe where they are in the process, and note their own progress towards recovery.

The chief consolation to offer Christians, however, is to widen their consciousness of God's mercy and compassion. Clinical depression is just as much a disease as any other illness, and people suffering from it are victims, not wilfully evil people. There is nothing to be ashamed of.

God does not hold against individuals any sins or mistakes committed when they were not responsible for their actions, or when the balance of their mind was disturbed.

Since the vast majority of suicides obviously fall into this category, this should be a major consolation to those families struggling with their grief.

No matter what human beings conclude, it is to be stressed that God knows the truth of every circumstance, and fortunately for us, His mercy is so much greater than ours.

(b) *Sudden death*

This includes accidental death, heart attacks and homicides. One feature that these circumstances all have in common is that they are more difficult to grieve than deaths where there has been prior warning.

Sudden deaths leave the survivors with a sense of unreality

about the loss which may last a long time. It is hard to believe that a person who died 'in good health', who was 'snuffed out in their prime' or who 'dropped without warning', is really not there any more. There is a great deal of unfinished business . It is not unusual for the bereaved to feel completely numb and walk round in a daze, not really being able to take in the fact that they have lost the loved one. They may not cry or face up to the loss for a considerable time.

When it comes, the kind of guilt is usually that of the self-blame and 'if only' type — 'if only I had been with him', 'if only I had not let him do that', 'if only he had had regular check-ups'. The bereaved have to face up to reality about this, and also to the fact that any reaction of strong anger they might have is quite normal. There is a natural need in these cases to blame someone — the inadequacies of the medical service, carelessness of other road users, friends who had led the deceased astray, and so on. In some sudden deaths there may have to be an inquest or even a trial, which adds to the problem if the judicial procedure is slow. Until the whole process is finalised, the bereaved are unable to let the deceased go, and so the grieving process can be long delayed. On the other hand, this is not always a bad thing. It can sometimes *help* the bereaved to arrive at the acceptance of loss when it all comes to its final conclusion.

Other features in cases of sudden death are the feeling of helplessness and frustration, and rage against the hospital staff or doctors or drivers or friends involved at the death. quite often God gets the blame — for not saving the person; the bereaved then also have to cope with their feelings of rejection of and hatred for God as well as the loss of the loved one.

The bereaved have many regrets for unfinished business, things they did not have the chance to say or do concerning the deceased. 'I never had the chance to tell him!', 'If only I had let him know I loved him!' 'If only I had not gone off the deep end like that, he would not have . . .' The best way to help in these cases is to try to find some way of 'closure' for this unfinished business, perhaps by talking quietly to the soul of the deceased as if he or she was in the room, and trusting that they will know your thoughts.

It is not really any consolation to say things like 'at least you've still got your husband/wife/children', or 'everything's going to be all right'. It *is* helpful, however, to let the bereaved come to acknowledge that the deceased really was loved and really is dead, and then to help them to see that they are not the only ones who have suffered these tragic circumstances – sudden death is no respecter of persons, it happens in lots of families. Death does not look around for the most 'deserving cases' to finish off in strokes or car accidents or railway disasters or plane crashes.

Christians should try to strengthen the faith of the bereaved, and bring them to accept the reality of the inevitable laws of nature which do not spare an individual, no matter how much loved or how worthy, from being crushed by the falling wall, shot by the bullet, or struck down by fatal disease. God knows every circumstance, and the most helpful thing is to allow the bereaved to feel loved by God, and that the deceased was and is also loved by God, even in these tragic circumstances.

One thing that I find helpful to the heart-rending questions 'Why him/her?' 'Why did God let it happen to him/her?' 'She'd never harmed a fly/done anything wrong/ had so much to give', etc – is to point out the example of Jesus himself on the cross. If anyone ought to have been spared a cruel death it was surely our dear Lord; and yet despite his agony in Gethsemane ('Let this cup pass from me' – meaning, 'please do not let me have to go through with this terrible ordeal' Mark 14.36) and his cry of horror on the cross ('My God, my God, why have You forsaken me?' Mark 15.34) – God did nothing to intervene to save him. He died in most appalling suffering.

The Christian should assume that if God was not prepared to save even Jesus from his pain and death, there is no logical reason why a lesser mortal such as our relatives should be spared.

Remember that after Jesus' despair in the Garden, he reaffirmed his determination to do God's will. 'Nevertheless, not my will but Thine be done' (Mark 14.36). God's will was for him to die. On the cross, after his cry of desolation, his last words before passing away were: 'Father, into Thy hands I commit my spirit' (Luke 23.46).

It is true that there are sometimes amazing and miraculous cures as the result of prayers of faith, and it is true that the history of the Church can provide plenty of examples of miraculous interventions on behalf of the saints – but by and large, there is no cure for death, and the important thing is the belief that death ultimately does not matter all that much, for one passes through it to new existence.

There are many interesting accounts of death experiences reported through people with mediumistic talents that suggest that people who die suddenly are hardly aware of their moment of death at all. Those who are shot do not hear the bullet that kills them, and do not feel it. Someone on whom a wall fell passed straight through it, and then watched helplessly as passers-by rushed to the scene and began to scrabble through the bricks for the battered body. Someone who died of a heart-attack while typing at her city desk merely looked up and saw a window with green fields and her mother (who had died long ago) coming across the grass. She got up and ran out to meet her, and only later realised that she had died, and had to be taken back to see her body slumped over the typewriter to be convinced that it was true.

Many bereaved people feel the loving presence of those who have died sudden deaths particularly strongly; it is as if they really do wish to say goodbye properly to their loved ones, and this awareness should not be disapproved or made light of – it can bring a great deal of comfort and strength to the one who has to carry on without them.

One word of caution, however, to spouses who cling on to the feeling that their deceased partner is still with them all the time. It is not disloyal if there comes a time when they begin to pick up their lives again without that spouse. Some people never remarry, and cherish their happy memories of dead loved ones until they, too, leave this earth hopefully to join them. But this is not always the case; many bereaved people eventually form new relationships and remarry – and they should not feel guilty about this.

It is worth remembering that our Lord was once questioned about a woman who had married seven different men; his reply was that in heaven there was 'no marriage, nor giving in marriage, but people are as angels' (Mark 12.25). Some people think it is impossible to really love more than one spouse, but this is not realistic. Remember, it is perfectly possible to love equally far more than one of your children; it is perfectly possible to love equally more than one man or woman – especially if these loves are separated by gaps of several years. This is nothing to feel guilty about, and if the 'dead' spouse is enjoying a happy afterlife in which the physical business of human marriage does not play any part at all, although it may be hard for the bereaved husband/wife to understand, that soul will not wish the remaining years of their spouses on earth to be spent as grief-stricken recluses who have turned away from all the joys of life.

(c) *Sudden infant death / cot death*

This kind of death occurs in infants under one year of age, usually between two to six months. By cot death, or sudden infant death, we mean the tragedy of a parent discovering a baby dead in the cot that had previously shown no sign whatsoever of being ill or in distress. The shock is horrendous, and feelings of guilt and despair excruciating.

The causes of cot death are not fully known, although there are lots of theories, but probably include accident and viral infections. Parents often conclude that their baby suffocated, choked, or had some previously unsuspected illness. These days, parents are advised not to lay their babies down on their fronts, as this might contribute to the number of deaths.

As the death occurs without warning, the parents are not at all prepared for the loss; and as there is absence of definite cause, there is considerable guilt and blame. It is only natural for everyone to wonder why the baby died, which inevitably casts the suspicion that somehow the parents really were to blame, perhaps by neglect.

The bereaved parents are also obviously in the state of being prepared for the baby's *life*, surrounded by the paraphernalia of childbirth and infancy – cots, nappies, baby clothes, toys, etc. It is a very sad task to have to collect all these carefully chosen and dearly-loved things up and set them aside, and turn from joy and delight in a new baby, to emptiness and grief.

As with other sudden death, there is a need for investigation, and often the police are involved. In these days of increasing child abuse and neglect, quite innocent parents are often put through the ordeal of being questioned and even held in custody – which inevitably adds to the stress.

A major factor to be considered in infant death which often goes overlooked is the effect on other children in the family. Parents should be very alert to this, for these brothers and sisters often suffer enormous guilt if they have previously been jealous of the new arrival, and wished they had not been born, or that they could get rid of them. Some of them even believe that it was their nasty thoughts that killed them, as if by magic.

The biggest cause of guilt for the parents is the 'if only' syndrome – 'if only I had been awake at the time', 'if only I had checked once more', 'if only I had not laid him on his face'. They need help to realise that it is quite unrealistic for a parent to be awake and watching twenty-four hours a day; their sleep is not to blame for the infant's death.

Sadly, because of lack of communication and guidance, there is often disharmony in the family afterwards when an infant dies; wives may feel that their husbands do not care enough about the death if they keep a 'stiff upper lip', and do not always cry when they do. The poor husband may be doing his best to cope with his own grief and a despairing wife by trying to calm things down and normalise the situation. He will sooner or later resent being accused of lack of concern or understanding. Inevitably mothers feel deep distress because they are so close to a child that has issued from their own body; a father should not be blamed if he cannot share the same maternal instincts.

Some women may fear renewed sexual activity in case there is another pregnancy and the experience is repeated. This puts a strain on many husbands which can result in tempers flaring and things being said that are hurtful. Many women suffer pressure from people who encourage them to rush into another pregnancy as soon as possible to make up for the loss. This may not be a bad idea, but pressurising people only adds to their stress.

Many women find the attitude of some well-meaning men that a baby is easily replaced, and one can have another one next year to make up for it, to be completely callous and lacking in understanding as regards the pregnancy, childbirth and short life of the dead infant. If bereaved women can accept that this attitude is normal in many men it may help to tone down their resentment towards them.

Sometimes, when a baby dies in hospital, the parents can be refused permission to be with the little deceased one, to hold it and love it in farewell. Sometimes the baby has to have an autopsy, and this can be very traumatic. However, the staff responsible for the autopsy can help a great deal if they can reassure the parents about the cause of the death; it is much easier to accept if they know it was nobody's fault but was inevitable.

Parents should be allowed full opportunity to grieve the loss of the little one, and to be assured that their innocent souls are safe with God.

(d) *Miscarriages and stillbirths*
Usually, when these tragedies befall a woman, everyone's first concern is for the mother and her health, and the miscarried or stillborn foetus is swiftly removed from sight and consciousness as if it had not been a real potential person with a soul of his or her own.

Some mothers are highly conscious of their unborn infants as real people, but frequently other people do not really regard them as separate individuals until they are actually born, and therefore they only focus on whether or not the woman will recover and be able to bear future children, and ignore completely her sense of loss.

Some take the point of view that if the baby was born dead, or only lived a very short while, the mother could not possibly have had long enough time in which to form any attachment or love for it – completely ignoring the relationship many women have with their children while they are still in the womb! The loss can be quite severe, even if others try to 'sweep it under the carpet' and minimise it in their attempts to cheer up the mothers.

The mother of a stillborn baby can experience a lot of self-blame – was it caused by unwise or violent exercise, over-eating or wrong diet, smoking, her husband's sexual activities? Husbands are frequently the target for the wife's anger – she often blames him for not having the same feelings, and as suggested in the cot-death section, if he is trying to be strong and supportive she may misinterpret this as 'not caring'.

Many husbands find back-up help from the doctor, who is frequently a man and may share the same point of view as the husband. It is worth repeating that it may be well meant, but it generally does not help the woman who has lost a child to be told that it doesn't matter, she should try again, and have another child as quickly as possible (rather like climbing back on to the horse as soon as possible after falling off). Although this may be quite realistic, if the woman s health is up to it, it strikes many women as being highly insensitive, and not what they want to hear at this time. These bereaved mothers have more awareness than the fathers of their unborn children as children, and should be allowed their time to grieve.

There is always a question-mark over whether or not to let the mother see the little corpse of her stillborn or aborted baby. Some people feel it is best removed tactfully, without the mother seeing it and being unduly upset by it; they feel that if he mother does not have any contact with it, she will all the more quickly put the tragedy behind her and start again. Others believe that seeing the dead foetus often helps to focus on the reality of the loss; but, hospitals do not always allow this, or only do it reluctantly.

When I had my first baby in hospital, the woman in the next bed to mine gave birth to a stillborn child which was instantly removed from sight. When the mother asked to see her baby I do not know what the outcome was for she was taken out of the ward – but the nurses behind her back commented very loudly that they thought it was 'absolutely disgusting!' and gruesome for the mother to have wished to have seen her child. The mother must have heard the comments, and been very upset. Luckily hospitals these days are becoming more humane, and many now allow the parents time to come to terms with the death and grieve with the little body.

Bereaved parents frequently find that people are uncomfortable about talking to them about their loss, and this does not help them resolve their grief. Sometimes family and friends are actually critical of their grief, and feel that they are making a fuss about nothing. It is *not* nothing; for the rest of their lives these women will know that they had a child (or children) that died, and will feel their loss.

It is important to realise that they have sustained a real death, and the loss should not be minimised.

(e) *Abortion*

Many people take a highly unsympathetic and cynical attitude towards women suffering bereavement due to deliberate abortion. Abortion is one of those socially unacceptable losses that people would rather forget, especially if the mother of an aborted baby was only a child herself, or unmarried. The surface experience of many mothers who had not wished for the pregnancy they have ended is usually one of relief and 'problem solved'; but a woman who does not mourn the loss of her unwanted child at the time may well experience great unresolved grief and guilt symptoms later.

Many women try to convince themselves that the foetuses are not real beings, but just part of their bodies. *They* have rights, but they do not consider the foetus to be a being that has rights. Guilt feelings based on the real existence of the unborn child will always surface later. Many women who have abortions are ashamed and in a state of panic, and once it is over they often feel that the best way to deal with it is to put it out of their minds as quickly as possible and pick up the threads of their life – but by doing this, they rob themselves of the grieving process and it will surface later. Some women do not think much about the children they stopped living until they are middle-aged; then, all of a sudden, they begin to suffer grief and wonder what those children might have been.

Sometimes the mother involved is only a young girl, and she has to cope with the anger, shame and disappointment of her own parents – partly because she got pregnant out of wedlock, and also because she then killed the baby which, after all, would have been their grandchild.

Many young girls are very ignorant about the process of pregnancy, abortion and childbirth, and have a feeling that they simply go to see a doctor, and it is all 'taken away'. They do not realise the risks, and how much they may suffer. Many teenagers do not want to talk about the experience or their feelings afterward. Some are traumatised and in a state of shock. Many are also in grief because they have been let down by the man who made them pregnant, whom they believed had loved them but who rejected them. If the abortion is of a first child, the young mother is frequently far more in grief over the man who has let her down and broken her heart than she is over the lost baby. This should not be despised and belittled; but the young woman should be helped to take a more mature overview of life and personal relationships, and responsible family planning, and a more realistic judgement of character when it comes to making future relationships. She may not actually grieve the loss of the aborted baby until many years later, when life has presented her with a longer view of 'might-have-beens'.

In an ideal world, no child should be born unwanted, or outside a stable relationship. Many parents of mothers who abort their children are very angry with them for having allowed themselves to get pregnant in the first place.

The bereaved girls need a great deal of gentleness, peace and sympathy to restore their self-confidence and hope in life. Those trying to give them help should not condemn or moralise, but give them a chance to talk out their feelings and face their futures realistically.

(f) *Anticipated grief*

A final category worth mentioning is that when grieving is done *prior* to an actual death. This is different from 'survivor grief'. If there is a long period of anticipation, the surviving relative begins the process of grieving in advance, and particular problems may arise. The most common is resentment at the 'burden' of caring for the dying person, which then leads to guilt because how could they have been so callous as to have lacked sympathy for their helpless relative? It is hardly his or her fault that he or she is dying.

The awareness of the inevitability of death alternated with the denial that the event is going to happen. There are a whole variety of feelings involved – an increase of anxiety, a freeing of emotional ties from the loved one. There is also a strong personal death awareness – as you watch someone deteriorate before your eyes during a progressive illness, you cannot help but identify with the process, having awareness that this may one day be your fate too.

When a child watches a parent die, they have the strong feeling that now they have moved up a generation, and are one step nearer their own turn.

People anticipating the death of someone frequently (and quite sensibly) practise 'role rehearsal' – 'what will I do with the children?', 'where will I live?', 'how will I manage?' This is quite normal and should not be thought wrong, but it can often be disapproved of by others who regard it as unkind and socially unacceptable behaviour to regard a dying person as if they were already dead. A person who talks about what they will do after the death is seen as insensitive, premature, and their comments in bad taste. Yet the worries are very real, and it is not wrong to make sensible plans.

The worst thing that can happen from the dying person's point of view is that the griever can withdraw emotionally from them far too soon, long before they have died. Sometimes relatives start to make plans for what they will do when the sick person dies, only to discover that they unobligingly do not pass away according to plan but live on and on; they begin to feel trapped, as if they dare not go anywhere, in case the invalid for whom they are responsible dies the minute their back is turned. Or, they might feel they are not allowed to make any arrangements for themselves until the person eventually does die, which inevitably leads to resentment, and then guilt for the resentment. It does nothing to help the dying one, either!

Sometimes the opposite can happen, and the family can move *too* close to the dying one, trying to overmanage the patient's care. Some go to the most extreme measures to keep a person alive even when the patient has reconciled himself/herself to dying, and wishes to be left in peace. They desperately seek all sorts of treatments, or pressurise them to undergo one operation after another, which can actually be quite distressing for the patient.

The best use of this time is in care of unfinished business – both in practical matters, and also in saying things that need saying. It is of enormous help if, instead of concentrating on impending tragedy, the persons involved can regard this as an opportunity to take care of things that need dealing with, let go of the strain and try to take pleasure in what is left of the life, and take the chance to put any disaffection right.

Don't forget that the dying one is also condemned to suffer from this anticipatory grief – the dying person is going to lose everyone, and the anticipation of this loss can sometimes be overwhelming. Sometimes they 'turn their faces to the wall' in order to cope with these feelings. It is a great blessing if the dying person has faith in the life to come, and the real hope and joyful expectation of meeting loved ones who have gone before, but counsellors should be tactful about mentioning this, in case the person feels they are being hurried out of this world.

Dying people should be tended with patience, gentleness, calmness, and a great deal of love.

A PRAYER

By the grace of Him in whose hands are all our souls, let us all learn to love each other and be more tolerant of our various shortcomings, praying to the Lord to forgive us our weaknesses and failures, and bring us the strength to regain our strong faith in Him. Let us try to bring light out of darkness, and to find new hope and a renewed sense of love for others out of the experience of suffering loss and bereavement. In the name of Him Who is the Compassionate, the Lord of Mercy. Amen.

9

Thinking about the Afterlife

Although many people profess to believe in God, sometimes they do not really feel it in their hearts. They have a mere opinion that God exists rather than that He does not exist. It has no significant practical consequences for them, and does not in any way affect the way they live their lives.

Others believe very strongly in the 'supernatural', but their beliefs are incomplete and unreliable, depending largely on hearsay, guesswork, intuition and superstition, and are based on subjective experiences.

Some people are obsessed by and engrossed in thoughts of the afterlife and its mysteries, others do not wish to confront it in any way whatsoever. However, whether eager or reluctant, every thinking person at some time or other is obliged to confront the deep, intriguing questions about the universe and our role in it, simply because we are aware that we are mortal. This seems to be the one basic way in which we are different from the other animals – we are all conscious of the uncomfortable fact that one day we will die.

Sooner or later everyone gets round to wondering whether the physical universe which we can see, touch, measure and know generally from the use of our senses, is all there is – or is there something more? Are our bodies just a 'bag of atoms' thrown together by chance, or little more than 'machines' – or do we have souls, are we 'machines with drivers'?

Where did we come from, and where do we go from here? Is everything just the result of chance, or is it rather the result of an integrated scheme and plan? Does human life have any meaning or significance, or are humans no more than perishable units that will cease to exist? Is there Someone in charge of it all? Is this life the only life, or will it be followed by some other state of existence, and if so, what?

Belief in the afterlife is probably one of the greatest motivating factors in human life. Its acceptance or rejection determines the very course of a human's life and behaviour. People who think this world is all that there is are obviously only concerned with their success or failure in it, even if they are good, unselfish people – but those who also believe in an afterlife which bears some relationship to the way we have lived and toiled here have a firm conviction that this later existence will give meaning and purpose to earthly life; they believe that their deeds and thoughts in this world affect the life to come.

The problem is that this realm of the afterlife is not available to discovery by the usual scientific principles. It is a shadowy land, 'beyond the veil', the 'undiscovered country from whose bourne no traveller returns'. It is not always contemplated with equanimity – some long to give up their struggle and go to the 'long peace of oblivion'; others yearn to go to Paradise and be close to God others, however, recoil from the very thought, and not just because they are wicked evil people. The speculations of religious people about what Heaven or Hell might be like has profound and varying effects upon us. There are many earnest souls struggling to live good lives on earth who would find an eternity of wearing white robes and singing hymns round the 'Throne of God' to be their idea of Hell!

Beyond perception

Fortunately the Bible teaches that not only does God truly exist – a unique Being above and beyond all the things He has created – but also that there is indeed a very great deal more to existence and the universe than that which we mortals can perceive with our limited and created senses. There is a whole realm which is not accessible to human awareness, nor bound by the limitations of the human intellect. It is utterly beyond human perception, and is in effect the Hidden or Unseen. Our known and witnessed universe is only like the tip of an iceberg – the bulk of which remains hidden from us.

Those who accept God as their Creator and Guide believe that it is patently obvious that nothing can come into existence from nothing, or exist without being caused. As Creator, God exists outside and beyond everything that He created; for example, He is outside Time, whereas all created things are part of Time. Things which are part of Time have beginnings and ends, but this is not true of God. There is a vast part of this creation which our human senses simply cannot perceive but which is nevertheless of vital importance to our existence. What is visible, and what we can perceive is probably only a very small and insignificant part of the totality that exists.

Believers also take it for granted that God's presence is everywhere, unceasing, untiring; but although people may strive to find Him, they can only 'see' as much as He wills. God Alone, as Creator, has the knowledge which is comprehensive. There is not one minutest speck of atomic existence about which He does not have full awareness, and – as regards human life – not one thought or aspect of our motivation which is not known to Him.

God is the centre of Reality – in fact, He IS Reality. He is the Creator, Sustainer and Provider, the one who creates what He wills in the wombs of mothers, gives a term of life to His creatures as He sees fit, and brings forth from the bodies that die that which persists in the afterlife.

He is Supreme, All-Knowing, All-Powerful – and also the Merciful, the Gracious, the Loving and the Forgiving.

Even so, He is the Unknowable. God is totally unlike anything any human can conceive of.

Yet, the great mystery that touches hearts and reduces even very tough people to tears is that even though He is so far removed from all our powers of understanding, a 'transcendent Being', nevertheless at the same time He is also 'immanent'. He is also inconceivably close to each one of us, He 'sees' us and knows our predicament, our sufferings and our joys.

In Christianity, belief in the Unseen is a prerequisite for belief in and understanding of God. One of the key concepts is that of forgiveness – that a human being has the opportunity to remove the terrible burden of guilt and sin by becoming aware of God's goodness, and seeking to find unity with Him. This, however, is not a matter of God imposing His will on us. God is consistent, and never-changing. He always loves His creatures that He has made, and it is not His will that any should go astray. Sadly, part of the 'deal' of being human is the fact that we have freewill, and therefore the ability to make wrong choices. Very frequently, we wander off. We have the choice to reject God.

When we do, we sometimes get into a situation where we actually deny God, and block His flow of love towards us. Jesus called this the 'unforgivable sin'. He said – 'I tell you, every sin and blasphemy will be forgiven humanity, but the blasphemy against the Spirit will not be forgiven' (Matthew 12.10).

It is not that God will not forgive a person's sins or shortcomings, but rather that if a person insists on refusing to accept His loving presence and 'puts up a wall' of wilful ignorance and blindness, refusing to recognise or accept the goodness and grace of the Spirit for what it is, then nothing can be really done with that person's mentality until the 'wall' is taken away.

Such concepts form the basis of Christian religious awareness, that this life is only a small part of a Reality so vast that the human mind can only grasp it in an extremely limited manner. Christians therefore automatically regard 'mechanical' and 'materialistic' interpretations of the universe as being inferior, false and misleading, especially in regard to the nature of human beings.

They maintain that although human beings are living, they are not themselves the 'real' individual – but God gave to each reproduced human form a quite distinct individual soul. Furthermore, it is not just that a human body *has* a soul; it is rather the soul, and not the body the soul lives in, that is the real person. The individual *is* the soul, and not his or her 'temporary and changing bag of atoms'.

'I was a handsome child, and it was my fortune to receive a good soul; no – I should rather say that *being* a good soul I came into my body undefiled, unspoiled. I saw that I could not expect to possess Wisdom unless God gave her to me' (Wisdom 8.19–20).

'Do not fear those who can kill the body but cannot kill the soul; rather fear Him who can destroy both soul and body in Hell' (Matthew 10.28).

Cycle of change
Faith in God and the Unseen turns materialism on its head.

Materialists think that matter alone is solid, real and enduring, and that immaterial or speculative 'things' like souls are just a figment of the 'imagination'; but those with a mind turned towards the Unseen propose that it is matter that is temporary and ephemeral and continually in a cycle of change and re-creation, and only the immaterial soul which is permanent and real.

It is therefore the so-called 'reality' of the human body which is the figment of the 'imagination', for it actually cannot keep itself 'the same' for two seconds running. Our atomic construction changes with every moment of our lives; our physical corpses are no more than a continuous chemical interchange of atoms with our environment (through food, breathing, etc), until the moment the soul ceases to 'organise'.

Moreover, Christianity – unlike Hinduism and Buddhism – teaches that each soul remains the soul of that individual person and does not travel into the body of another human, or animal, or live again on earth in future reincarnations. (It does not claim that it *cannot*, only that it does not – this is not the plan). The doctrines of reincarnation propose that there is a fixed number of souls moving endlessly up and down the scale of worthiness with an infinite number of chances to get things right through these reincarnations. Judaism, Christianity and Islam, the three great revealed monotheistic systems, are more stark – you live once as your test, you die once, and then, even though you still live as a soul, you are not permitted to return to earth.

There is an afterlife of quite a different system awaiting each individual, and there is a gulf, a partition, between this world and the world of souls. Souls are not intended to come back to their bodies, except, perhaps, at the time of Judgement. There are no millions of chances.

'There was a rich man, who was clothed in purple and fine linen, and who feasted sumptuously every day. And at his gate lay a poor man named Lazarus, full of sores, who desired to be fed with whatever fell from the rich man's table . . . and the poor man died and was carried by the angels to Abraham's bosom. The rich man also died and was buried; and in Hades, being in torment, he lifted up his eyes and saw Abraham far

off and Lazarus in his bosom. And he called out, "Father
Abraham, have mercy upon me, and send Lazarus to dip the
end of his finger in water and cool my tongue, for I am in
anguish in this flame". But Abraham said, "Son, remember
that you in your lifetime received your good things, and
Lazarus in like manner evil things; but now he is comforted
here, and you are in anguish. And besides all this, *between us
and you a great chasm has been fixed*, in order that those who
would pass from here to you may not be able, and none may
cross from there to us." And he said, "Then I beg you to send
him to my father's house, for I have five brothers, so that he
may warn them, lest they also come to this place of torment."
But Abraham said, "They have Moses and the Prophets; let
them hear them." And he said, "No, father Abraham; but if
someone goes to them from the dead they will repent." He
said to him, "If they do not hear Moses and the Prophets,
neither will they be convinced if someone should rise from the
dead!"' (Luke 16.19–31).

The teaching of Jesus

(Many scholars, incidentally, would see in this above Passage a
reference of Jesus to his own resurrection, and the sad fact
that those who have already got 'their eyes closed' are not
likely to alter their position because of the teachings of
Christianity.)

Thoughts about what happens after death are many and
various. Some pious people look forward to actual bodily
resurrection, and believe that although corpses break down
after death, a person's body and soul will eventually be reunited
when the hour of Judgement comes, although the resurrected
body will be quite different from the earthly one.

'Thus says the Lord God to these bones: Behold, I will cause
breath (or spirit) to enter you, and you shall live. I will lay
sinews upon you, and will cause flesh to come upon you, and
cover you with skin, and put breath (or spirit) in you, and you
shall live; and you shall know that I am the Lord' (Ezekiel
37.5–6).

Others believe that the 'life-form' which is to come is as

different from the mortal as the fully-grown plant is from the seed.

'Some will ask, "How are the dead raised? With what kind of body do they come?" You foolish man. What you sow does not come to life unless it dies. And what you sow is not the body which is to be, but a bare kernel . . . so it is with the resurrection of the dead. What is sown is perishable, what is raised is imperishable . . It is sown a physical body, it is raised a spiritual body' (I Corinthians 15.35–37, 42, 44).

Whatever one's thoughts, once the possibility of life after death enters the consciousness, a second factor comes along with it – the teaching of Jesus and the other great religious prophets about the *point* of human earthly existence; all revealers of God teach emphatically that there will ultimately come a Day or Time of Judgement, when our human lives will be reviewed in detail, and different fates will await us according to whether we passed or failed to develop certain characteristics.

Many religious people also insist that certain fixed beliefs have to be developed too, but this was not the actual teaching of Jesus. He never, so far as we know, demanded adherence to any complicated creed; certainly not the creed of the Christian churches of any century following his own earthly life. Instead, he insisted (like his Jewish forbears) that humans were to 'love God with all their heart, soul, mind and strength', and to 'love their neighbours as themselves' (Mark 12.29–31). There were only two other commands left by Jesus – to 'love one another' (John 15.12), and to 'do this in remembrance of me' (I Corinthians 11.24 – the symbolic meal of sharing bread and wine).

Entry into the Kingdom of Heaven, he taught, was based on how you *lived* and not so much on what you *believed*. People get all sorts of beliefs and ideas into their heads, many of them quite wrong and terribly divisive. It is all too easy to spend a lifetime enslaved to a wrong belief; the test comes when we are required to 'love the neighbour that we have seen' rather than make speculations about God, whom we have not seen. (See that much-neglected epistle, James, chapter 3!).

Once one believes in the possibility of the Day of Judgement and the future life, then the great task of every human being is to prepare for it by bringing all the various facets of their complex natures into a smoothly functioning, harmonious whole – and in order to do this, humans have to exercise the power of their will and govern their physical bodies and emotions according to the laws which God laid down for their wellbeing. Only when they are 'at ease' with God and their consciences can humans achieve a synthesis, integration and balance.

By using freewill, humans exercise judgement between right and wrong, and have capacities for thinking, transmitting knowledge, feeling and acting which have not been given to other creatures. However, limited human minds cannot comprehend the Unseen. The true nature of God and the mysteries of the Hereafter are not given to us to know – despite the revelations, and attempts to describe the indescribable in symbolic language.

10

The Importance of Life Before Death

God is infinitely beyond anything which the mind or senses of humans can grasp or comprehend or imagine or explain, and far, far beyond having any similarity to anything He has created. In short, God Most High has not the least resemblance to the limited semi-human 'gods' created by human minds with all their imperfect knowledge and understanding, invented to supply the deficiencies in their comprehension.

Yet, obviously, God is intimately concerned with His creation; His existence has absolute relevance and meaning for every single human being. God is involved in every part of His creation from the vastest of stars to the minutest of atoms which comprise them – for His concern is not only in creating but also in sustaining, directing and guiding, and as regards human beings, in giving them the direction necessary for living their lives in this world in such a manner as will ensure them everlasting good in the life to come.

The 'freedom' of life without belief in God is really enslavement to one's own ego, or to other human beings, or to their ideas and values. The service to God 'whose service is perfect freedom' consists of being free of servitude to anything or anyone other than one's real Maker.

Faith gives humanity a glimpse of the reality of another life of a very different nature from the life of this world, a life in which we shall be completely transformed, so much so that we cannot understand it, no matter how hard we try.

Some people doubt the reality of this afterlife, but they are in a state of ignorance. The 'logic' of materialistic science insists that since after death a person is reduced to dust, and since no person has ever witnessed a case of revival of a destroyed corpse, therefore death and destruction *must be* the end of life, and there is no life after death.

But is this really scientific reasoning? Not if you have an awareness of the Unseen. Even if not one single person has ever seen a case of revival, it means only that they can state with certainty that *they do not know what will happen after death*, but not that nothing will happen. Science tells us nothing – negative or positive – in this respect, and the assertion that life after death has no existence is totally unfounded. Just because nobody has seen it, does not mean that something has no existence. No person, not even humanity in its entirety, can claim this. The universe is full of all sorts of things that humans here have never seen or could imagine. And, as it happens, there ARE many people who claim that they can give bits of 'circumstantial evidence' about the afterlife, as we shall see.

Change of attitude

When people become conscious of the existence of God it alters their entire attitude to life. The person no longer wanders blindly, but becomes aware that the universe has a meaning, and that each individual plays an important role in it. To believe in God and then live badly is a nonsense. Once we are aware that God knows all and sees all, how can we deliberately act in a dishonourable manner?

It is meaningless to claim to love God and then lie, cheat or hate. Real awareness of God brings with it the submission to Him of all one's thoughts and deeds. It is obvious that someone who has lived throughout their earthly life with the correct awareness of Reality is in an entirely different inner state from one who has lived with an incorrect or distorted view, or in forgetfulness, rebellion or ingratitude.

No person who has tried to live a good life, believing in God, need be afraid – even if they are haunted by fears that they might have failed. Thankfully, it is not the judgement of any human that will judge us.

Human beings have a perverse tendency to be 'well thought of' if not to 'be superior' which often manifests itself in the urge to judge others – usually to knock them down and point out their wrongs and failings. Jesus taught:

Judge not, that you be not judged . . . Why do you see the speck that is in your brother's eye, but do not notice the log in your own eye?' (Matthew 7. 1–5)

No human being is so merciful and compassionate as our dear Lord, who knows all the background motives for our actions that we may not even know consciously ourselves, and if we sometimes fall, every single thing will be taken into account We need not fear Hell even if we have sinned – to imagine that any human being could possibly be perfect is an arrogant nonsense.

How, then, can we achieve forgiveness if we have done wrong, or failed? Thanks be to Him, it is not a difficult thing. If a person is truly sorry, all they have to do to gain God's forgiveness is to ask for it. God *always* forgives the true penitent, even if other human beings, the self-righteous, do not!

This is the key teaching of Jesus' beautiful parable of the Prodigal (or Spendthrift) son. This youth took his inheritance early from his father, and went off and wasted it on worthless pursuits. When he became penniless and ended up in the gutter, he decided to go back home to ask his father's forgiveness.

'While he was yet at a distance his father saw him and had compassion, and ran and embraced him and kissed him' (Luke 15. 20).

The parable then goes on to tell of the reaction of the youth's elder brother, a devout and worthy son who had never done anything but his duty. Being human, he found it impossible to forgive and welcome back the stupid boy – until his father made him ashamed by showing his great love.

Does God forgive people all the time, then, no matter what they have done? What is one to make, if that is true, of all the hints about Hell?

Belief in a 'time limit' in which one can seek and receive forgiveness is an important part of awareness, and this is no secret thing. In every generation God has sent witnesses or messengers to stir consciences and warn people of the reality of it, even though many might like to believe that God will ultimately forgive everything. The three monotheistic faiths teach that if people choose to reject the warnings and not believe in God's principles and live according to His wishes –

when it so obviously right to reject unkind and depraved living and do one's best to live well – then that is their free choice and their character is fixed. Just as the people they hurt had to bear the consequences of their unkindness in this life, they must accept the consequences of their actions in the next life.

Facing judgement

All three monotheisms teach that people will 'taste death'. Their souls will leave their bodies, and their corpses will rot away and their atoms go back to replenish the soil from which they were taken. However, what happens to the souls during this time is one of the unknown mysteries for which there are numerous theories but no proof. Whether they 'rest' or are highly active, for example, is a matter of subjective belief.

In the end, Judaism, Christianity and Islam teaches that all will ultimately stand before God, each one to face their judgement for which they have been personally responsible. They suggest strongly that all our actions, our words and motives, are the raw material for this judgement in which we have unconsciously (or maybe consciously) written the verdict for ourselves.

According to these faiths, it is what we do with our lives *now* that determines what happens to us in the Hereafter. Without this judgement after death, this world would be a world of almost total injustice, with the sinners winning all the way. In one of his most beautiful parables, Jesus taught that it *does* matter how we live:

'Before Him will be gathered all the nations, and He will separate them one from another as a shepherd separates the sheep from the goats; and He will place the sheep on His right hand and the goats on His left hand. Then the King will say to those on His right hand, "Come, O blessed of my Father, inherit the kingdom prepared for you from the foundation of the world. For I was hungry and you gave me food, I was thirsty and you gave me drink, I was a stranger and you welcomed me, I was naked and you clothed me, I was sick and you visited me, I was in prison and you came to me"' (Matthew 25. 31–46)

The 'sheep', bless their hearts, were such good and modest people that they did not even realise they had done it; and the 'goats' protested that they had never seen him and had therefore not been given the proper chances. Maybe these were people who had spent all their lives 'serving God' by pointing their noses directly at their concept of Him, and ignoring all that went on around them. I expect we have all known people like this – wonderful at prayer and preachifying, but mean and malicious of heart. Said Jesus, 'inasmuch as you did it not to these the least of my brothers, you did it not to me'. And so the 'goats' go away into eternal punishment, but the righteous into eternal life'.

Jesus, therefore, suggested clearly that those who denied God and rejected His guidance, who devoted themselves to selfish living without caring for others would be consigned to an abode completely alienated from God – inevitably fearsome and terrible, a state of enduring torment from which there would be no respite.

They will long to have another chance to return to earth to try again, in the light of their newfound knowledge of Reality, but it will be too late. On the other hand, a state of unutterable bliss and serenity awaits those who left this life in a state of surrender to Him.

Most religious scholars, taking into account all the insistent teachings that God Himself declared these things to be beyond our knowledge or understanding, regard all the descriptions of the afterlife, including such things as perpetual youth, beauty and so on, to be understood symbolically, since in eternal life the faithful are not subject to physical limitations at all, but 'are as angels in Heaven' (Mark 12. 25)

There is little direct teaching in the New Testament about the afterlife, but the above quotation comes from an incident in which Jesus was asked a direct question by the Sadducees (who did not believe in the survival of the soul). They intended to make a fool of him. They asked who the husband of a woman would be in heaven, if she had married seven times. Jesus replied:

'Is not this why you are wrong, that you know neither the scriptures nor the power of God? For when people rise from the dead they neither marry nor are given in marriage, but are *like angels* in heaven. And as for the dead not being raised, have you not read in the book of Moses, in the passage about the [burning] bush, how God said to him, "I *am* the God of Abraham and the God of Isaac and the God of Jacob"? He is not the God of the dead, but of the living' (Mark 12. 24–27).

God of the living

This teaching was born out earlier by the unique incident of the Transfiguration, the account given in Mark 9. 2–8. On this occasion Jesus took three of his closest disciples, Peter, James and John, up a high mountain – and they suddenly saw him shining with white light and conversing with two 'ghostly' figures who were identified as Moses and Elijah. These once living characters had not become 'evil ghouls' or angels with wind and harps, or puffs of smoke, and neither had they continued to age. Although Moses had died sometime around 1350 BC and Elijah around 820 BC they both still existed as Moses and Elijah, and they were able to see and communicate with Jesus while he lived on earth.

All we can really say about the afterlife is that it is a completely different dimension, and we are created afresh in a form beyond our knowledge, although we can probably assume that God will not suddenly require us to give in to all the desires, lust and wealth and gluttony and inequality that we were taught to avoid as mortals! To be in Paradise must be to live in a state of perfect peace, healing and love, unimaginably better than this life, and not at all boring. All the old rivalries of family, tribe, nation or culture will no longer trouble us – they will be healed for ever and forgotten. There will be no more bereavement, pain or suffering.

'God Himself will be with them; He will wipe away every tear from their eyes, and death shall be no more, neither shall there be mourning nor crying nor pain any more, for the former things have passed away. He who sat upon the throne said, "Behold, I make all things new."' (Revelation 21. 3–4).

What about the question of being reunited with our dearly-loved ones in the life after death? Some believe strongly that we will meet again with our loved ones, and find their worn-out selves made fresh and new. Others think that the family bonds of this lifetime do not necessarily continue, since individual eternal souls outside time are not bound by the relationships that belong to the world of time. That could be very good news for couples whose marriages were not so good.

'In any case, the wish to prolong a marriage into eternal life has about it just a hint of possessiveness that marks, and often spoils, human relationships. "I want you all to myself" is a frequent expression of human love. In terms of the perfect community of Paradise it is very excluding. After all, many people have never had access to one of these satisfyingly exclusive relationships. Are they to be deprived again, for all eternity?' (*What happens after death?*, D. Winter, p. 30).

Maybe all old relationships of the present world will be dissolved. Maybe it is not that our relationships will be wiped out in Paradise, which might be a contradiction of love, but that there will be no more exclusive relationships, and our relationships with God will purify and perfect all other relationships. Maybe we won't want to keep people to ourselves there, but will see people as our brothers and sisters, close to one another because we will then be all close to God.

No individual has the right to believe that he or she is guaranteed Paradise, or that they can deduce which other people are destined for Heaven or Hell. Only God has full knowledge of this. There may well be some surprises. As I suggested earlier, some very religious people can spend a lifetime enslaved to totally erroneous beliefs.

'Not every one who says to me 'Lord, Lord' shall enter the Kingdom of Heaven, but he who does the will of my Father who is in Heaven. On that Day, many will say to me, "Lord, Lord, did we not prophesy in your name, and cast out demons in your name, and do many mighty works in your name?" Then will I declare to them, "I never knew you; depart from me, you evildoers!"' (Matthew 7. 21–23).

The more conscientious and devout a Christian is, the more likely to be aware of shortcomings and weaknesses. Therefore, knowing that only God controls life and death, and that death may come at any moment, they try to live in as perfect a way as possible, doing good deeds and thinking good thoughts, so that they can in a way 'send on ahead' such things as will merit the pleasure of their Lord, and look forward to an afterlife in the hopes of His mercy and grace.

Christianity encourages people not to fear death, but to accept it with patience and resignation as an inevitable part of our life process, and to keep in our minds the happy notion that 'death' is not the end of existence.

This awareness keeps the whole of earthly life, whether intensely happy or in deepest pain, in perspective. Earthly life is passing, temporary, and only a test for the future.

11

The Compassionate God

God heals us as individuals from all those things which hold us back from living a new life of reconciliation, our grief and guilt. Those ills may be of the soul – God heals by forgiving our sins, and enabling us to allow that forgiveness to flow out to others, and not least of all, to ourselves. He heals by mending hurtful memories or anxiety caused by stress, irrational guilt, fear, and all the psychological upsets which disturb our peace of mind, and this, In turn, allows our physical bodies to be healed of the symptoms of their physical distress.

We have to realise that God does not *want* us to suffer. He wants us to be healthy, happy and wholesome. People learn to trust their lives to God, because they trust that ultimately everything is in His hands. The deepest form of healing will always be the forgiveness of sin, the putting right of our relationship with God.

Some people, unfortunately, look on the Creator-God as a Judge who is on the look-out to punish severely the tiniest fault, rather than as Supreme Compassion and Grace. Fear, not love, sin not grace, life not death, dominates their spiritual consciousness. Their religion is sometimes learned by rote from teachers, so that they may have the answers to all the questions, but God has never become real for them in their hearts – even though they might win the prizes for religious education!

Deep down, they are terrified about the state of their souls, believing themselves to be terrible people not worthy of God's mercy, and literally terrified of Hell. They have missed a very important part of religious understanding.

Yes, it is true that God approves and disapproves of certain things for which He has given clear guidelines in the Bible and which can also be deduced from the life of Jesus. But it is *not true* that any believer should take a superior stance over other people's apparent failings, or assume that any lapse from the 'straight path' will automatically land anyone in Hell. This is not what Christianity teaches at all.

It is not for anyone to make 'righteous' assumptions about which of us are destined for Heaven or Hell. No matter what things may seem on the surface, no one but Cod knows who has really accepted His offer in their hearts, and who rejected it. Only God can possibly know the destiny of any human spirit, and we are pretending to *be* God if we start declaring who is and who is not acceptable to Him.

Hell is a reality rather than a place. Those who reject God and His morality have cut themselves off from all that is good, loving and true. It is a 'place' in a negative sense; it is where God is not.

Use of free will

It is not God's purpose for *any* human being to end up in Hell. The only beings actually consigned to Hell are the devil and his angels – those evil forces and powers that spoilt God's perfect world. But if people use their God-given freewill to reject God's offer of forgiveness, then it may well be that they will share that terrible fate. But if they do, it won't be God's choice, but theirs.

The kind of people we are talking about here are not those who fail or fall short in some detail of the high standards – but people who are literally determined to be evil and go against God. All the other sinners, the weak, those who have given in sometimes to temptation and then are sorry, the negligent, and so on – *all* are forgiven by God the moment they ask forgiveness. And they *will* ask, because they are not of those who have denied God in their hearts. This does not excuse wrong behaviour or practice; but it is important to realise that God's compassion is greater than any human person's.

For that type of Christian trapped upon the treadmill of trying to regulate every least detail of their lives in case they go to Hell, God is not the Supremely Compassionate One by any stretch of the imagination, but a cruel and vindictive bully waiting to catch them out. They need an insight to give them a completely new way of thinking and acting – their fear of God is the wrong sort of fear. God is both Justice and Perfect Love. Those who refuse to meet God's conditions have good reason to fear Him, but those who have grown up in the atmosphere of His loving-kindness know that there is no doubt that their repentance will be accepted. Christians, therefore, should not adopt the attitude of servile fear, like guilty servants fearing their Master's wrath, but what we might call a *filial* fear – that of loving sons and daughters who want above everything else in life to do what their Father wants.

True Christians live at peace with themselves, because their lives are saturated by the healing power of God. They make His teachings their way of life.

Unearned love

Believers are always expected not to fear death and pain, but because they are humans this is sometimes unrealistic because faith falls short, and then the rebuke from those not touched by grief and loss becomes another unnecessary and cruel cause of suffering. No matter how fervent our faith, God has not stopped us from being human. Grief may be a sign of weakness, but it is not a sin. God does not punish us for the times when our strength fails us, only for the times we lose our physical control and do something evil without repenting for it.

One of the great obstacles to healing is the feeling in some religious people that they deserve to be punished because they do not really love God as they should, and do not merit His love. Yet God's love is completely unearned – we can *never* merit it by our own unaided efforts. If a Christian has the sense of guilt to such an extent that they feel God *cannot* forgive them completely, this is wrong faith. They *say* God is Compassionate and Merciful, but they are not *believing* it in their hearts. They fear God, and stand in awe of His might, His power, His holiness – but somehow the realisation of His love evades them.

It may be because the person has never known the human love of a father. One finds deep inner damage in people who suffer from an unhappy childhood where they were the victims of selfish, demanding, possessive parents – no matter how 'religious' they might have claimed to be. These people often grow up hating themselves, and because of their inner feelings of resentment towards their parents, they are unable to relate to God as a God of Love and Mercy. The chain of 'damaged' people as a result of inadequate parents often goes back many generations, as any psychologist knows.

The false attitude to forgiveness which sees God *only* as a vengeful judge has done untold damage over the centuries. When we make fear of punishment in this life and the next the chief motivator in religion, it means that the soul is so shrivelled, the mind so tormented, and the body so suppressed, that God cannot 'unlock the door' of our hearts, bolted by fear, which we can only open from the inside. We need true faith to set us free.

It is love of God which unblocks the coldness, bitterness, the ache of bereavement, the pain of loneliness and rejection, the resentment at our illtreatment by others, and the thousand other things that keep us so locked up we are unable to love even ourselves.

Jesus' wonderful acts of healing were essentially proofs that God loves us and wants us whole and healthy. His headings were not so much miracles as 'signs' or 'works' given to him to do by Our Father in Heaven, in Whose name and power he accomplished them. He healed because he loved, and because these people needed it.

It didn't matter whether the hurt people had great faith in God or not; it didn't matter whether or not they deserved healing, or were saints or sinners – Jesus had the same attitude of love and forgiveness towards them, and wished only to bring them peace by bringing them close to God once more.

Any person should be able to learn from this how much God cares and is concerned for the sick, the sufferer, the dying, the dead, and the bereaved.

The beginning of our forgiveness and healing is love of God. Once we believe in our hearts that He loves us and wants us whole, and takes no pleasure whatsoever in the thought that by our own stupidity and perversity we might end up in Hell – then we remove from our lives the obstacle of fear which destroys our trust in Him. He loves us all individually, even to our fingerprints! He knows us better than we know ourselves.

Sadly, not every believer remains true to their calling – too many are led down the road of self-righteousness and exclusiveness. God's love is not conditional – as if He will only love us if we do this or that; God's love for us does not ebb and flow – it is unchangeable. It is *our* love, and *our* response that is fickle and it is a tragedy that so many Christians feel that because they may have done something which estranged them from God, that He has in consequence distanced Himself from them. This is not true – God never ceases to love us, no matter what we have done; we have only to turn back and be sorry, and His forgiveness overflows.

God's love is unchanging even when we change for the worse and forget Him. Even though we may think we are worthless, God thinks the opposite, especially when we have no-one to love us, not even ourselves! He never ceases to love us. When we sin, it is we, and not God, who put up the barriers. It is not true that we have to spend the rest of our lives in penitential acts and prayers, trying desperately to appease Him and 'soften Him up' – that is the sin of despair, and *not trusting God.*

Those who stress the wickedness of sin without emphasizing also the limitless mercy and forgiveness of a loving God do a grave disservice to Him. They are trapped in a bog of self-condemnation and are limiting the mercy of God to their own narrow dimensions.

Christians who constantly harp on about guilt and sin are not building up repentance but a whole load of neuroses in those they should be helping. Many negative-thinking people believe that the world today has lost its sense of sin. Maybe, it has lost its sense of forgiveness – a forgiveness which is the result of real faith in God and love of Him.

These Christians are so slavishly afraid of God that they are afraid to love Him. Fear is basically a lack of faith and hope. People who live in fear of God do not really believe deep down that He has the power to help them or change them or maybe they think that He does have the power, but doesn't care anyway. Fear of failure soon gives rise to depression and anxiety – but faith and hope give us courage to face up to ourselves and to life. What God says to us is much more important than what we say to Him!

Once we get our relationship with God right, the rest falls into place; and the test of the sincerity of our repentance will always be whether or not we in turn are ready to forgive those who have hurt us.

12

Grief and 'Religion'

Does a person's 'religion' make any difference to the way they experience death and grief? It depends on the understanding of religion. There are healthy attitudes to religion, and there are unhealthy ones. Some religious attitudes help life to grow, and some stunt personality growth.

Unhealthy religion is usually centred about the denial of responsibility. It projects a concept of the universe and a God who is open to manipulation, capricious – like an oriental despot. Believers with this sort of attitude often act quite seriously as if they genuinely believe that if they cry loudly enough or long enough they will be able to 'bring themselves to God's attention', make Him notice their 'worthy cause', and perhaps even make Him act differently in accordance with what they want Him to do. They seem to expect that if they are devoted enough, or chant enough charms, or do enough pious practices, God will produce cosmic results, and violate the law and order of the universe just to oblige them.

All their prayers and incantations might seem very pious, but their attitude is really one of *lack of trust* in the will of God. God does not need to be told our problems – He knows everything already. He will not have failed to observe that one of His servants is sick, or dying, or bereaved.

God is not there just to oblige us – no matter how worthy we are, or desperate our cause. God is pure Love, Light, Power, Spirit and Truth. These are the uncommitted power-sources of creation waiting to be spiritualised and used by the God-aware individual, and this involves no game of trying to manipulate God for personal favours. That would really be a form of sacrilege. The true believer has to develop the quest for inner perfection and dedication that is willing and able to function within the laws of God's universe, for all those purposes which are in accord with His will.

God is not a cosmic errand-boy. He is not standing by, waiting for our orders of the day – sometimes with the implication that He had better get on with doing what we want or we will punish Him by rejecting Him. This is a real trivialisation of the nature of God, and yet we find so often people who lose their 'faith' in God because He did not seem to do what they wanted him to do – and let a loved one die.

Stand in faith

True religion enables us to take charge of our own lives and live with responsibility in a disciplined way, which reduces the causes of guilt and understands the wise processes necessary for the management of grief.

Some bereaved people feel that they are so helpless to cope with life that they need a special dole of 'cosmic kindness' to get them through. Sometimes religious leaders misguidedly speak in terms that seem to promise more than is reasonable, and this can lead to disillusionment and a further retreat into unproductive religious practices.

They do not need to crawl through life begging for what is already theirs – God's love and caring concern, and their duty towards Him. They have to stand in faith, and accept it.

While they may not like the results of a molecular process or a violation of the law of gravity, or the war that follows from political failures, they would not want to destroy reality by asking God to do what is a violation of His nature. We cannot tempt God to do our will. It is important instead to discover how to bring our lives into close accord with that ultimate will.

Death seen in terms of a capricious universe with a God who should do our bidding is painful and depressing; death seen when we understand the meaning of life in a larger context is seen in a totally different light. God's plan for the universe is much larger than the individual, and we should grow to realise that.

It may be that life is as short as that of a moth, or as long as that of a sequoia tree; what matters is not its length but its quality.

Our religious faith should help us find a perspective through which we can evaluate our own feelings and the ultimate reality that we would not deny. Healthy religion moves beyond the denial of responsibility, the distortion of reality and the creating of illusions. It puts death in perspective. It helps us to understand the meaning of the pain that comes with some death and is absent in others. It undergirds life with an adequate philosophy, emphasizes the reality of life, and the forms of love that continue to sustain life.

Only physical things die; spiritual things already have the dimension of the infinite and eternal and are therefore indestructible.

Death tosses the human being into spiritual turmoil. One of the biggest problems for devout believers is the attitude of so many friends, who – because of their faith in the afterlife – simply do not seem to see that there is a problem, or if they do, refuse to admit it.

'You are a committed Christian; your family are committed Christians. Christians know there is nothing to fear about death – therefore we can all be quite sure that you will cope wonderfully!'

You may not, but because of the attitude of these 'comforters' you cannot speak up or make it known that you need help. In fact, religious people who speak like this are quite possibly trying to escape their own emotional involvement, that they feel embarrassing or unable to handle. Nobody knows what to say for the best to a bereaved person – and in fact, a companionable silence is often preferable to false platitudes.

Well? Should Christians not grieve at all? Should they just accept a terminal illness as God's will, or a test of faith? What can they expect from God? What should they ask Him for?

It is not wrong to ask questions. Human beings are creatures with minds and rational faculties. If God had wanted automatons with no minds, He would have created us that way. It is all right for us to ask the reasons; but we cannot demand an answer. Sometimes one is given, if it is necessary for us to know. At other times we simply have to accept that there *is* an answer, although God has not given it and since His dealings with us are always loving and for our ultimate good, we can leave the matter there. This is where faith comes in.

What does life offer to a Christian? A life free from guilt?

Possibly, if they try hard. A life free from the fear of death?
Possibly, if they have enough faith. A life that can be lived
differently from that of nonbelievers? True, with God's help. A
life free from sorrow, problems and difficulties? Sadly, no.

Being a Christian does not protect anyone from the reality of
suffering. Belief is not some kind of spiritual inoculation which
will provide immunity from all that is difficult and painful.
We love God – but doesn't He care when we suffer? In times
of crises, it is so easy to feel that He is far away and cannot
hear our cries – but this is not so. His love will never desert us
or let us down, even in our darkest hour.

Promise of comfort and strength

It is not wrong to grieve. People who believe in God grieve for
all sorts of things, including the callous and hard-hearted
attitudes some people have towards one another, and at the
mess that human rebellion against God has made of His
world. People with sympathetic hearts feel human misery
deeply; some work to exhaustion to heal the sick and reach
out to the needy. To see someone we love suffering makes us
unutterably sad, and God knows that. He gave us the feelings
in the first place.

But believers should not grieve in the same way as those
who have no hope – for God promised His people comfort
and strength right into the valley of the shadow of death, and
beyond.

'The Lord is my Shepherd; I shall not want; He makes me
lie down in green pastures. He leads me beside still waters. He
restores my soul. He leads me in paths of righteousness for His
name's sake. *Even though I walk through Valley of the Shadow
of Death, I will fear no evil; for You are with me.* Your rod
and staff comfort me ... Surely goodness and mercy shall
follow me all the days of my life, and I shall dwell in the
House of the Lord for ever' (Psalm 23).

When Christians really make up their minds to turn their
lives over to God, they become quite sure that they have
the support and backing of their Lord, a certainty that
makes them firm and strong. No amount of difficulties,
impediments, hostile opposition, misfortunes or tragedies can

make them give up their resolve! Their faith inspires bravery in them.

There are two things which make a person cowardly. Fear of death and love of safety, and the idea that there is someone else besides God who can take away life, and that people, by adopting certain devices, can ward off death. Belief in God purges the mind of both these ideas. The first idea goes because they know that their lives and property and everything else really belong to God, and they become ready to sacrifice all for His pleasure. They get rid of the second idea because they know that no weapon, no man or animal has the power of taking away their life; God alone has the power to do so. A time has been ordained for them, and even all the forces in the world combined cannot take away a person's life a moment before the appointed time. It is for this reason that no one is braver than the one who has faith in God.

Many people wonder why, if God is all powerful and loving, He does not cure our loved ones of cancer, or prevent wars and famines, etc – either directly through miraculous intervention, or indirectly (perhaps through medical science?).

God sometimes works through suffering. Some people are physically healed, others are given the ability to live with the illness and finally to die with trust and hope. Suffering can never be considered enjoyable, but there can be good responses to it. If we see that neither distress nor death can separate us from the love of God we have a living hope which transcends all the trials of our present situation.

A responsibility

As believers, who try to accept God's will, should we fight the disease, or accept it? Would it be right for a patient to refuse medical treatment on the grounds that it must be God's will for them to have this disease, and therefore to fight it is wrong?

The Christian answer to that must surely be 'No'. Such apathy is against the general desire of God to see us always working for healing, wholeness and peace. We have a responsibility to care for our bodies as best we can – so we should encourage the patient to seek and take medical advice and cooperate with whatever treatment they think is right; they should move towards full health as positively as they are able.

But a Christian will always have to acknowledge that the final outcome is in God's hands. If we pray for our sick and dying, and for the bereaved, it is never wasted; God always hears us, and something always 'happens' even if it is not quite what the person has prayed for. We are human and limited in our understanding. Instead of telling God what we want, we should try to ask God what it is He wants for us, or wants us to do, in this situation. Sometimes He gives a very clear indication of what it is He wants us to do – through inner conviction, through a verse of the Bible, or an insight given through another person.

When we are less certain, we can pray for what seems to be the best solution, acknowledging that God's wisdom is perfect.

We are not specks of dust drifting in space blown by random destiny. We are each of us unique – no two people are alike, not even identical twins. Each one of us is born for a specific reason and purpose, and each one of us will die when we have accomplished whatever it was to be accomplished.

True healing is not necessarily a cure, but a completion of God's work in body, mind, emotions and spirit.

There is a danger in accepting too literally the symbolism of God as some kind of 'super' human being, an almighty 'Father'. This can easily confuse us as to the nature of God. We all have our own ideas of what a good father is like – we know he would be fair, kind, just, loving and forgiving We know that a good father help his children when they are in need, disciplines his children, does not let them run wild. We know that he takes time to care for and be interested in his children.

Earthly fathers often fall short of this ideal, of course. If our own fathers were less than perfect, our concept of God could therefore be influenced by imagining a 'male' God who was angry, vengeful, and unforgiving. A weak and ineffectual father, or a father who is too busy for his child, can distort in a person's mind the character of the perfect and sovereign Creator of the universe.

We cannot understand perfection, or sovereignty. Our finite minds are limited – but God is not.

Will remain a mystery

Death sometimes leads us to question things we had taken for granted before. Does God really exist? Does He love me? How could He let this happen?

God welcomes honest searching. Truth stands out clear from error. It will not collapse under investigation. Ask your questions, seek your answers. Ask for the wisdom that will lead you to Him. Search for answers – find out for yourself what the Bible says about the things you are questioning. You may find yourselves coming to a new level of commitment, one that is perhaps meaningful for the first time.

But you will have some questions that cannot be answered, because God chooses not to tell us everything. Many, many things will remain a mystery in this world. God has given us enough information so that the most intellectual person can be satisfied yet He leaves enough out so that we must all have faith without fully understanding.

Don't worry; instead, pray, and tell God your needs, and don't forget to thank Him for His answers and His blessings. If you do this you will experience God's peace, which is far more wonderful than the human kind can understand.

Don't waste your time with cries of 'if only'. Regret is a wasted emotion; it is futile, for we cannot go back and change things around. No amount of self-recrimination can change the past. Of course you have made mistakes – we all do that, and some of these mistakes have heavy consequences. So long as you did the best you could at the time, that is as much as you can do. Don't be pre-occupied with regret. If you did or said something wrong, confess it to God, and accept His forgiveness. Bring the entire situation before God, commit it to Him, and leave it there.

True believers have nothing to fear in the most gloomy scenes of life; they have nothing to fear in the valley of death; they have nothing to fear in the grave they have nothing to fear in the world beyond. For God is with them. They do not go anywhere alone – for God is the Companion, the Guide.

Dying people *seem* to enter the final valley alone. The

friends accompany as far as they can, and then they must give the parting hand. They can cheer the dying ones until they are deaf to all their sounds; they can cheer them with their looks until their eyes become dim and they can see no more they can cheer them with a fond embrace until they become insensible to every expression of earthly affection, and then they seem to be alone. But dying believers are *not* alone. Their God is with them in that valley, and will never leave them. On His promises they can depend, and by that Presence they can be comforted, until they emerge from the gloom into the bright world beyond. All that is needed to dissipate the terrors of that valley is to be able to say 'You are with me'.

13

Entering Life

Our knowledge is only like the tip of an iceberg; the most part of what there is to know is hidden beneath the waves, unknown and unimagined. People who give help to she bereaved often use one or two helpful similitudes about the Afterlife to aid them in their healing work. God has allowed us to see several 'signs' or symbols' in the natural world around us, which help us to widen our conscious awareness.

The ants

My friend Beryl Statham was once an inquisitive child, watching in fascination a column of ants going busily about their business in her garden. Suddenly she had a flash of insight.

'I suddenly became conscious of a colony of ants in the grass, running rapidly and purposefully about their business. Pausing to watch them, I studied the form of their activity, wondering how much of their own pattern they were able to see for themselves. All at once I knew that I was so large that, to them, I was invisible – except, perhaps, as a shadow over their lives. I was gigantic, huge, able at one glance to comprehend the world of the entire colony. I had the power to destroy or scatter it, and I was completely outside the sphere of their knowledge and understanding. They were part of the earth, but they knew nothing of the earth except the tiny part of it which was their home.

Turning from them to my surroundings, I saw there was a tree, and the sun was shining. There were clouds and blue sky that went on for ever and ever. And suddenly I was so tiny – so little and weak and insignificant that it didn't really matter at all whether I existed or not. And yet, insignificant as I was, my mind was capable of understanding that the limitless world

I could see was beyond my comprehension. I could understand
my lack of understanding . . . Would a Watcher think me to be
as unaware of His existence as I knew the ants were of mine?
He would have to be vaster than the world and space, and
beyond my understanding, and yet I *could* be aware of Him, in
spite of my limitations . . . Because there was this glimmer of
understanding, the door of eternity was already open. Running
indoors, delighted with my discovery, I announced happily,
"We're like ants, running about on a giant's tummy!" No one
understood, but that was unimportant; I knew what I knew.'
(*Angels in Dark Places*, B. Statham)

The ants helped my friend to understand that our awareness
of the universe, and the things Unseen, is probably only as
limited as an ant 's view of our world, and maybe less so. This
realisation – a child's sudden insight – altered the shape of my
friend's entire future life and attitude both to God and to the
Life to Come.

The seeds

St Paul was one of the leading early Christians who was
almost a contemporary of Jesus, and who knew several of his
disciples personally. When writing specifically about the question of the resurrection of the body at Judgement Day he used
the similitude of seeds being sown in the earth.

'If the dead are not raised, let us eat and drink, for tomorrow
we die . . . Come to your right mind, and sin no more! Some
have no knowledge of God. I say this to your shame. Some will
ask: "How are the dead raised? With what kind of body do they
come?" Foolish people! What you sow does not come to life
unless it dies. What you sow is not the body which is to be, but
like a bare kernel, perhaps of wheat or of some other grain. But
God gives it a form as He has chosen, and to each kind of seed
its own form. For not all flesh is alike, but there is one kind for
humans, another for animals, another for birds and another for
fish. There are bodies of heaven and there are bodies of earth . . .
So, with the resurrection of the dead – what is sown is
perishable, what is raised is imperishable. It is sown in dishon-
our, it is raised in glory. It is sown in weakness, it is raised in

power. It is sown a physical body, it is raised a spiritual body . . .
the "first man" was from the earth, a man of dust; the "second
man" is of heaven . . . just as we have born the image of the man
of dust, we shall also bear the image of the man of heaven. I tell
you this, brothers, flesh and blood cannot inherit the Kingdom
of God, nor does the perishable inherit the imperishable.

Lo! I tell you a mystery. We shall not all sleep, but shall all
be changed, in a moment, in the twinkling of an eye, at the last
trumpet. For the trumpet will sound, and the dead will be
raised imperishable, and we shall be changed. For this perishable nature must put on imperishability, and this mortal nature
must put on immortality . . . Then shall come to pass the
saying that is written: "Death is swallowed up in victory." "O
Death, where is your victory? O Death, where is your sting?"'

(Corinthians 15. 32–55)

Nobody, looking at a seed held in the hand, could possibly
imagine what sort of plant or tree it would grow into – huge
oak tree, delicate orchid, humble blade of grass? So it is with
our bodies. They are just like tiny seeds – in the Afterlife our
forms may be as different as the plant from the seed we may
become 'huge oak trees' or 'delicate orchids'; it is not given to
us to know.

The seed is placed in the earth, where it splits open, and out
of it comes forth whatever beautiful and wonderful form God
has already programmed within it – and the dry husk, no
longer needed to contain it, will simply be cast aside. So it will
be, brother and sisters, with ourselves and our loved ones.

Tadpoles and frogs

Another similitude that can be very helpful, especially when
talking to bereaved children, is that of the tadpole and the
frog. The tadpole is such a tiny little wriggling thing, confined
to living all its life in water. If you were to show a tadpole to
someone who had no knowledge, and tell them that it will one
day change into a totally different creature, with a different
body and the freedom to roam at will about the earth, and
then ask them to draw what that creature might perhaps look
like – it is almost certain that nobody would think up the idea
of a frog! Or that you could take a similar tadpole, and it will
change into a newt – different again. Or another similar

creature, and it will change into a caddis-fly and inhabit the
skies! And yet it is so, and human beings no matter how young
can observe these changes for themselves and draw a lesson
from them. Here we are but tadpoles ... there, who knows
what will be the result of our metamorphosis?

The human can also consider how difficult it would be for
an adult frog to convey to an infant tadpole what life was like
outside the environment of the pond. The tadpole has no
knowledge or experience of it, and cannot possibly imagine
what it must be. The tadpole may not even be aware that it is
going to become a frog!

The caterpillar, cocoon and butterfly

Let us take another similitude, one that is very helpful when a
person, especially a child is actually faced with the fact of
death, and perhaps has to see the deserted body of a loved one
to make farewell before a funeral.

Consider the life cycle of a butterfly. Like the tadpole, the
butterfly starts off as a completely different creature with a
totally different set of circumstances and environment. What
use to tell a caterpillar, crawling around a leaf, that one day it
will cast loose and soar in the freedom of the skies? There is
no way the butterfly can convey information about its life and
what it sees to the caterpillar, clinging with its sticky feet to
the twig.

And before this miraculous change takes place, there is
another stage. The caterpillar enwraps itself in a shroud of its
own making, the chrysalis or cocoon. It is quite a good idea if
a child with no knowledge can receive a demonstration of this
somehow perhaps in the normal course of events long before
they have to come to terms with bereavement.

There is the cocoon, a silent, still and apparently lifeless
thing. Yet inside it is a free spirit and there comes a moment
when the cocoon is split and cast aside, and out of it emerges
the most beautiful creature, the butterfly. Before you know it,
it spreads its wings, and flies away into the vast sky, a wider
world than your own. So it is with our own bodies and souls.
The seemingly dead body is no more than a cocoon, ready to
be shed and cast aside by the beautiful spirit within so when
we look at a body, we are not seeing our loved one, but only

their 'empty shell'. And although we will miss that person for a while, what reason is there to grieve?

The mortal remains of our loved ones will go back to being the earth of which they came, until such a time as God sees fit to call them out again and reform them and we have His promise that He can restore anyone he wishes in full detail, even to their fingerprints. Meanwhile, the souls of our loved ones will fly away to experiences we cannot know now.

These are happy thoughts, full of consolation, hope and joy.

Live every day as it comes

Yet, finally, brothers and sisters, let us remember that our times are unknown to us; they may be short or long – we have no way of predicting. It is no use expecting to be able to put off to tomorrow what we ought to be doing today. That tomorrow might never come. If we are believers, we know that whenever we say of a thing 'I will do it later', we must add 'if God wills!'

People who have had personal contact with death find that it changes their awareness of life. Conscious awareness brings with it a new appreciation of life. I have a personal similitude of a beautiful set of cups and saucers. They were given to me when I got married, and I put them aside 'for best', saving them up for some future occasion. After twenty-three years of marriage my life changed and my husband and I were divorced. Unpacking my cupboards and discovering this marriage-gift which had never been used was one very sad detail of this experience which taught me a lesson. My time of marriage came, and I had received the gift; then before I knew it, the time had gone but the gift was still unwrapped!

Life *before* death is important. Let us try hard to live every day as it comes, accepting each new dawn as a fresh gift from our dear Lord, full of opportunities and chances to do good and kind things to those we love. Let us not waste our time, or find ourselves called back to God with His gift 'unwrapped'!

If we are angry or disappointed with someone, help us to love them more, and try to change the situation. If we are impatient with someone, give us the grace to remember that You are pleased with snails and tortoises just as much as race-horses and greyhounds. If we are short-tempered with some-one, help us to find patience and sympathy.

For one of the hardest things bereaved people have to face is their guilt – the many 'if only's, the many times they have said things that should not have been said, or not said the things that should have been said; done things that should not have been done, or not done the things that should have been done.

Help us to live every day *as if it was our last*. Help us to accept each new day as a gift, and not to waste it. Help us always to use our time to love, and to bring peace, and to heal, and to reconcile, and to work hard for the bringing of Your will on earth. Help us to love and appreciate those who You have given to us, and to cherish them while we have time.

Help us to accept them, knowing that we might not have chosen ourselves the particular character given to our brother or sister, or parent or child, but that this choice was not ours to make, but Yours. If a relative distresses or disappoints us, help us to love them *more* and not cast them aside and then regret it later.

A PRAYER

Help us always to remember You that we may dedicate our lives to Your full service – not out of any fear, but out of love for the One who is Most Perfect, the Lord of the Unseen, the Lord of this life and of the Life to Come. Amen.

Words of Consolation

I love you, my children, and I hold your lives securely in My hands. I will not let either of you fall, nor let you go through anything you cannot cope with. I have My reasons for this trying time. Although they may seem obscure and unseeable now, in the future you will be able to look back and see My hand clearly working for you in your lives.

As you look at the blackness before you, be prepared to go through it into the bright sunshine. Have courage, because I am beside you. I have gone before you and I follow behind. My protection is yours.

I gave you life, and now you must be prepared to surrender your life and all you possess into My hands. Do not hold anything back; have confidence in Me, for I am beside you.

Although you cannot see what lies ahead of you, and your path is strewn with boulders, I hold your hands and I will lead you gently. I know your pain and fears. Trust me, I weep with you and I will laugh with you. I know what I am doing. I LOVE YOU. (Adapted from *The Long Road Ahead*, W. Green)

Bibliography

Abulafia, J., *Men and Divorce* (Fontana, 1990)

Ball, M., *Death* (OUP, 1988)

Brown, E. and W. Green, *Somebody I love has died* (Lion, 1990)

Buckley, M., *His Healing Touch* (Collins, 1987)

Davidsen-Nielsen, M. (see N. Leick below)

Green, W., *The Long Road Ahead* (Lion, 1985); also see E. Brown
    above

Greaves, H., *Testimony of Light* (Neville Spearman, 1969)

Grey, M., *Return from Death* (Arkana, 1985)

Innes, D., *How to mend a Broken Heart* (Lion, 1991)

Israel, M., *About Death* (CFPSS, 1977)

Jackson, E.N., *The Many Faces of Grief* (SCM Press, 1977)

Kubler-Ross, E., *Living with Death and Dying* (Souvenir, 1982)

Leick, N. and M. Davidsen-Nielsen, *Healing Pain, Attachment, Loss
    and Grief Therapy* (Tavistock, 1987)

Moody, R., *Life after Life* (Bantam, 1976 and L.A.L. Inc, GA)

Morse, M., with Perry, P., *Transformed by the Light* (N.Y. Villard,
    1992)

Moster, M., *Living with Cancer* (Hodder, 1960)

Pearce-Higgins, J.D., *Life, Death and Physical Research* (Rider, 1973)

Pincus, L., *Death and the Family* (Faber, 1976)

Riemer, J., *Jewish Reflections on Death* (Schocken Books, N.Y.,
    1974)

Ring, K., *Healing Towards Omega* (N.Y. Morrow, 1984)

Sheppard, G., *An aspect of Fear* (DLT, 1989)

Statham, B., *Angels in Dark Places* (Churchman Publishing, 1990)

Stevenson, V., *Love after Death* (Corgi, 1980)

Stroud, M. *Face to Face with Cancer* (Lion, 1988)

Watson, D., *Fear No Evil* (Hodder, 1933)

Watson, L., *The Romeo Error* (Book Club Associates, 1974)

Wilson, I., *The After-Death Experience* (Sidgwick and Jackson, 1987)

Winter, D., *What happens after death?* (Lion, 1991)

Wright, C., *Living Through Grief* (Lion, 1960); *Living and Dying*
    (Lion, 1991)

Zaleski, C., *Otherworld Journeys* (N.Y. OUP, 1987)